It's Me, Not You: How I Survived Toxic Work Environments

PORSCHA JACKSON, PHD

Published in the United States of America by

Paisley Publishing, Houston, TX

Hardcover ISBN: 979-8-3431398-1-5

Paperback ISBN: 979-8-9911022-0-9

Ebook ISBN: 979-8-9911022-1-6

Cover Design: Andrew McCray

DEDICATION

To my past self, with love

CONTENTS

ACKNOWLEDGMENTS

In all thy ways acknowledge Him and He will direct thy paths. Proverbs 3:6

I am extremely thankful to know my purpose and to be able to operate in my God given gift; therefore, I must first give thanks to God for His plans for me and the wonderful desires of my heart that have and will come to pass.

Sarah Ban Breathnach said "Real life isn't always going to be perfect or go our way, but the recurring acknowledgement of what is working in our lives can help us not only to survive but surmount our difficulties." For that reason, I must acknowledge my mother and my friends Tatum and Alicia for rendering support, encouragement, and honesty to me during some of the most difficult of the difficulties I expressed in this book. Thanks for reminding me of who I was and not letting me succumb to a lesser version of myself.

I also must acknowledge all of the people and personalities who are mentioned in this book. Whether you meant to or not, you have influenced my life in a positive way, taught me lessons I will never forget, broke me down so that I could be built up, and guided me to my purpose. Without our season this book does not exist, so for that I am grateful and wish each of you the best and God's amazing grace.

Lastly, I must acknowledge JLB for his mentorship, Andy who always has me covered, and my family and friends who constantly believe in and support me.

PREFACE

God works in mysterious ways! As a little girl, I never dreamed of being an author, I didn't even like reading, let alone writing. However, I've always been a good student and throughout the years have found life to be my greatest teacher. I still cherish the wisdom I received from elders as a child and the worldly knowledge from friends and those who I thought were friends as I became an adult. My experiential learning in the workforce and my spiritual awakening of the present have formed a journey that has centered me on a lifelong path of learning and meaning-making. This book is a demonstration of this process.

The concept of this book, "It's Me, Not You!: How I Survived Toxic Work Environments" came to me at a time when I was realizing the purpose for my life. The irony was the book was an epiphany to me but the content had already written itself through 11 years of work experience. The only thing waiting was the connection to academic research, which I received in graduate school after leaving one of the most toxic environments I have ever experienced. This is what I mean when I speak of the mysterious ways of God.

The seed had been planted when a man at a New Year's celebration at church told me I would be an author. My immediate thought was *he has no clue what he's talking about* but after a few seconds, I reflected on the message that was given by our pastor and said "I receive it". Acknowledging that prophetic statement and the act of calling those things that are not as though they are, is a first step to moving forward to God's grace and what He has predestined for us. Sometimes we have to pay attention to the *word* and not the messenger, again God works in mysterious ways and uses us all, even our enemies. An example of my spiritual growth is not immediately saying "no" but saying "yes Lord, I submit to whatever you have for me" no matter the delivery or the messenger. God can use your enemy to help you or even the last suspected person or a terrible experience.

The title of this book is based on a presentation I did in my psychology class some years ago. We were given the assignment to do a presentation on psychological disorders we had read and discussed in class. A lover of psychology (I would read the chapter before class and after class and study class notes because I didn't want to miss anything), I was able to recognize some disorders in my current work environment. Therefore, I did my presentation on three personality disorders of three people I worked with and titled the presentation, *It's not them, it's Psychology*. From this title derived my mantra for work, "It's not them, it's me" a phrase I had been secretly using to cope with my strange and frustrating experiences with my co-workers. I would blame myself for being sane in an insane work environment for reasoning why I was having bad experiences at work.

From the psychology class, I realized these people justifiably had a psychological disorder (according to the textbook and not by a licensed professional). Knowing their disorders, I found ways to deal with them according to their alleged disorder. This became my saving grace as I was now able to maintain my sanity in such a toxic and exhausting work environment. Prior to my class, I was dealing with co-workers as if they were 'sane' and that established the toxicity I was experiencing through our interactions. However, all along these people were facing psychological challenges and needed to be handled according to their individual challenges. So essentially, it WAS me…it was me not knowing the right solution.

The lesson is when things aren't going smoothly, look at yourself. What you want to   consider is who you are dealing with and make appropriate adjustments if you want to have some sanity; otherwise, you will be the newest convert to the insanity team. The saying goes "if you can't beat them, join them"; however, I invite you not to join them and use this book to help you decide differently.

There was a story I read once in a Spanish class that basically told the lesson, *if you argue with fools, no one can tell the difference.* In fact, Proverbs 23:9 states *words to a fool will help him to despise such wisdom.* Therefore, this book will help you make a difference, have understanding, inner peace and distinguish you from the fools you work with through the sharing of my personal experiences (in a satirical way) and researched solutions.

The following chapters will tell of actual experiences and encounters I've had with former co-workers, my reaction, how I should have handled it, and how you can overcome these same situations on your job. Though my experiences are unique to me with specific place, time, person(s), and perception, the gist of the stories are universal and I bet you can relate in some way to these experiences. Remember, it's not the actual people we are up against but the powers and principalities that rule (Ephesians 6:12). I'm confident we've gone up against some of the same personalities. If not, either you haven't worked long enough or you have been truly blessed to work with some great people…and for that I'm jealous! Just kidding, these experiences allowed me to grow and mature as a person and a professional and now I have the great opportunity to help others by sharing my stories. Enjoy!

P.S. The names in this book have been changed to protect the persons of whom I speak. In fact, they've been given nicknames that categorize their behavior at the time of my interaction with them and have no relation to their actual personal identity (Table 1).

Table 1: Toxic Environment Behavior Pseudonyms

Blockhead	Conny	Contortionist
Circus performer creates illusion of hammering objects into their skull. In toxic environments, their extreme stubbornness makes communication difficult.	A toxic individual who engages in con artistry under the guise of being a business woman.	Toxic individual, like the circus act, is able to maneuver themselves in & out of tight situations by telling narratives to benefit themselves with little to no consideration of others.
Creeper — A person, sometimes confrontational, who constantly watches others with the intent to intimidate, agitate, and destroy.	**Dr. War** — Battling internal conflicts, projects their insecurities & punishes others to feel superior, using past experiences to gain respect by making others feel inferior	**Emmy** — Drama queen/king, who comes across engaging but their melodramatics result in office chaos from their overacting and demand of attention at any cost.
Floral — A highly toxic individual who behaves in a multitude of ways with the belief someone is out to get them.	**Geppetto** — Enabler who operates as a puppeteer providing ammunition for toxicity to exist instead of using their influence to diffuse toxic behaviors and patterns.	**Harlequin** — A sophisticated office clown who acts foolishly to please and fit in with the most powerful crowd.
Ice Queen — A mean spirited person who has a negative attitude and shuts everyone out.	**Liesa/Lyla** — Individuals who lie on a consistent basis to protect themselves.	**Medusa** — Beautiful person who reveals themselves as rage-filled, marked by blatant lying, selfish ambition, & ruthlessness, like a Greek myth.
Pretender — Individual who pretends to work but lacks skill set for assigned tasks and in turn engages in other activities while on the job.	**Shaydee** — Person who intentionally misrepresents themselves in an attempt to trick others into doing things as a result of having an ulterior motive.	**Snake Charmer** — Someone who earns the trust of others for the purpose to manipulate them to do their dirty work to make themselves appear blameless.
Squatter — Masquerading as a model employee, they do just enough to meet expectations until finding their next opportunity.	**The Ringmaster** — A person in a leadership position directing toxic behaviors and performances in an organization.	**Tightrope Walker** — Like the classic circus act of balancing oneself on a narrow rope, this individual engages in a balance of their manipulative behavior and a professional facade.

1 PRETOX

I have never been one to know what I was supposed to do in life from birth. I relish in the stories of those who felt their calling from the beginning and spent their youth defining their dreams. My childhood friends would boast about being doctors, lawyers, veterinarians, nurses, teachers, models, hair stylists, dancers, and professional athletes. I would witness them going to recitals, practices, doing each other's hair, and playing out their dreamed profession during recess. Often I wondered how they came to know those professions and who told them they were obtainable. Who made the decision?

I remember being told I was smart and to "get good grades", "I only want to see A's and B's from you" my uncle would say as he told me I could be anything I wanted. At that age, I did not understand the power of that statement or the statement itself. In school, teachers glorified astronauts, doctors, and lawyers, all of which I personally knew nothing about. Sure, I went to the dentist and doctor twice a year but I did not see any on a regular basis. If these careers were so great, how come none of my teachers pursued them? How come no one explained the path to these amazing professions? Why were these professions and professionals so distant from my reality? How does my good grades get me to my "anything"? What my environment showed me were housewives, retirees, retail and factory workers, and teachers, whom I only saw at school. My mom worked at a bank and I would shadow her on Bring Your Daughter to Work Day but I never really understood what she did; however, I saw she worked hard but was underpaid, just like all the other adults in my world.

Throughout my childhood, teachers often told us we should have a role model. I struggled with this because I really did not look up to anyone. I respected people but never saw anyone whose career I wanted to pattern myself after. Maybe it was the scorpio and only child in me that called me to always want to be myself, someone different and just do my own thing. I did not have any older siblings but I had older cousins who acted as my protectors in public and my agitators in private. My teachers were never a contender because they were adults who went to school every day just like I did. Besides, they boasted about careers they did not have.

I was not sure what was available to me, so under duress I sought to find a role model. Television was a great teacher for me back then (and still is) and I remember being consumed with the U.S.A. Track and Field Hall of Famer, Florence Griffith Joyner. She had these long fingernails, like me, but hers were polished with flamboyant designs. She was pretty with long thick hair (that I wanted) and always had fashionable and custom-made tracksuits. Her grace and style on the track distinguished her among her fellow competitors, yet she was quiet and humble, like me. Though track was not the profession I really desired, I subconsciously took a page from her book and gained a secret confidence that I could do things my way.

Consistently, like everyone else, I was asked the adage question "what do you want to be when you grow up?" I had no clue but quickly learned "I don't know" was never an acceptable answer. How dare I, a child of six years old, not know what profession I would have at the age of 25, 26, or whenever, which seemed like a galaxy of years away. I soon began to fall in line and just say "veterinarian" because my friend told me. I later asked my mom what "veterinarian" meant and quickly realized I had no intentions of doctoring sick animals because it literally, to this day, breaks my heart to see an animal in pain. Besides, I don't even like touching sick people, so this was never my dream but I went with it until I reached adolescence. At that point, "I don't know" was an expected and accepted response; however, it became a mystery to me that I secretly sought to solve.

I was always mature for my age, so adults trusted me a lot. I was never ushered out of the room when they talked about "grown folk business". Perhaps because I was quiet and at times went undetected, so I heard and saw things other children didn't but I handled it all in stride. I was a natural observer, responsible, and could follow directions well. People automatically trusted me, so I soon became a babysitter, making consistent pay watching my two younger cousins in the summer while their mom went to work. I had to wake up early in the morning and would sometimes miss out on playing with my friends because I had to do my job from 6:30am-3:30pm, but at least I got paid. However, as much as I loved my cousins, I knew childcare was not in the cards for me.

When I got to high school, my first job was in food service and then in telemarketing. Food service paid me $4.25 an hour and though I was earning money when my friends were not, I quickly realized that once I turned 16, better money-making opportunities that didn't require me to wear a corny uniform, stand on my feet all day, and work as hard awaited, hence my entrance into telemarketing. Plus, I could get school credit for going to work and could leave school early to do it...it was a dream come true. I would soon miss the food service's free food and fun environment but at 16 years old I felt it was no longer cool.

During high school, my career aspirations naturally went to the area of business because I was a working girl. I was good at saving and allocating my money, so I gravitated to accounting but I was notorious for making simple mistakes that would cause me to start the ledger all over again. I soon moved on to marketing. This seemed like a natural fit to me because I was basically a couch potato and could recite commercials, make up my own commercials to sell fake products, and persuade most to buy something after telling them about the product I learned about on television. I would go around the house singing commercial jingles and making my own jingles for just about anything. I remember telling my mom how Tide could improve their commercial with my soulful rendition of their jingle and comical skit. My ideas were good, so I thought, but they never saw the light of day. However, I would later major in marketing in college and continue to rely on the convenience of telemarketing to get me through graduation. It was during that time, I would get my foundation in management and a small taste of the not so fun side of the work environment.

As a telemarketing lead and a quality assurance representative, I enjoyed the benefit of not having to take phone calls but earned the responsibility of evaluating the calls of others. It was a flexible job with decent pay for the number of hours I worked. However, dealing with the attitudes of some of the telemarketers could make my day unpleasant. The nature of telemarketing itself did not require a great skill of any sort, so it attracted your brightest and dullest and had tremendously high turnover.

My biggest challenge was with some of the oldest and youngest employees who did not respect my authority because they felt I was too young. I would later realize that some people in those groups, frankly, did not respect authority at all, regardless of age, gender, or race. Despite the push back of a few, I became well-respected at that workplace and soon promoted to manage the off-site facility during the peak seasons.

This promotion became a blessing and a curse. It would give me great problem-solving and people skills. There were so many different types of characters who called themselves employees, yet I was flexible and understanding to handle them all. However, it began to take a toll on me. I remember one time after conducting a performance appraisal on a known difficult employee, I went to my car just to find it keyed. I guess that would explain why she kept glaring at me before disappearing then returning with a conspicuous smirk on her face.

Then a change in management imposed strict rules on telemarketing leads that required phone duty in addition to an increased workload. The attitudes and the lack of work ethic among the newest employees soon became overwhelming, as the lead on-the-job trainer. The environment became a little hostile and suppressive, to the point I vowed to leave shortly after my college graduation. I just couldn't take it anymore, it felt like I was going to a dungeon every time I would report to work. I said 'once I earned my degree, I would and should not have to put up with that type of work environment', so I quit one month before my sixth anniversary and a payout of vacation time.

Telemarketing became my introduction to a toxic work environment. The sad part was I had no idea it would be the beginning to several unpleasant work environments I would come to endure. I would later experience harassment in the retail industry from female department and store managers because of my age and education. This would prepare me for the biggest workplace lessons I would ever learn about management, survival, office politics, and myself. The highlights of these amazing experiences are captured in the forthcoming chapters of this book as I take you through my eight-year journey as an employee at an organization, I affectionately refer to as "The Circus", and some side gigs along the way. This would begin my true understanding of toxicity.

Foundation of Toxic Work Environments

A toxic work environment is simply defined as an unhealthy environment that is damaging to those who work there. Dysfunctional and stressful interactions are normalities to this type of environment. The toxicity, as experienced daily, often forces employees to skip work and become defensive and protective of themselves instead of focusing on the success of the organization.

This environment is not something that just appears but develops overtime, many times having roots in the culture of the organization funneling from the executive level and branching out through departments to trickle down to the frontline employees. Toxic work environments are largely those where poor communication, corruption, and high turnover reside. The atmosphere is tense causing: unnecessary stress, unclear expectations, unrewarded hard work, unacknowledged ethical behavior, unenforced policies and procedures, and non-transparent practices.

The mentioned characteristics are often caused by the lack of communication through the management levels and between departments, supervisors, and employees. With no examples of accountability for mistakes or performance of those in leadership positions, an environment that breeds skepticism and lack of trust is soon created. This is sometimes acted out in nepotism, promotion bias, micromanagement, and various forms of discrimination. The leaders of these types of environments are the typical narcissistic personalities who use manipulation tactics, resulting in negative and inconsistent communication and unfair practices.

The toxic environment may not include all of these characteristics and depending on your level of involvement in the organization, may not be visible to the outside eye. However, if this description of a toxic environment resonates with you on some level or is identifiable in your department or fellow colleagues, then toxicity may be brewing in your workplace. A toxic environment can go undetected when you are new and are already disconnected to the organization. Sometimes you may not realize your environment is toxic until something unpleasant happens to you, despite seeing it happen to others. Other times you can misdiagnose your environment based on typical symptoms you may experience because of displeasure or dissatisfaction with areas of your life.

I did not realize my environments were toxic until I started paying attention to my changed behavior. I hated going to work and in doing so would unapologetically show up late and developed a lackadaisical outlook on my job performance. I felt unappreciated, micromanaged, and exhausted from a series of negative experiences with colleagues and management. Some employees have negative physical and mental health effects from toxic work environments, including emotional and relational effects. Figure 1 will help you to better assess whether you are in a toxic environment.

Figure 1: TOXIC WORK ENVIRONMENT CHECKLIST

Here is a comprehensive list of characteristics of a toxic work environment. A workplace that has a few of these characteristics does not necessarily designate a toxic environment, but a combination of the majority of these characteristics on a consistent basis could mean you are in a toxic work environment.

- Poor Communication
- Personality Disorders
- Nepotism
- Discrimination
- High Turnover
- Low Morale
- Cynicism
- Bullying
- Racism
- Sexism
- Abuse-verbal, physical, emotional
- Glass Ceilings
- Sexual Harassment
- Hostile Work Environment
- No Rewards
- Lack of Appreciation
- Culture of Ostracism

While I do not wish toxicity on anyone, it probably was the best thing to happen to me, professionally. I learned a lot about myself and it gave me great stories to share in this book that will hopefully help you to thrive in your workplace. "It's Me, Not You" provides some of the mistakes I made in my professional career and how I learned from them. Each chapter discusses a survival technique while using my personal experience to illustrate the point. Again, the names have been changed to illustrate the behavior and not the person. As I hope you will understand it is the type of behavior you are dealing with and not the person themselves. When you are able to separate the two, you are on your way to understanding the basic principles of surviving in a toxic workplace.

2   IT'S THEM

Fresh out of college, I had a great job, it didn't pay much but I enjoyed working there. Good people, occasional free food, flexible hours and boss, laxed dress code, and overall positive environment. There was a sense of freedom there, as long as you completed your work in a timely manner, you were good. Everyone was like an extended family member, no one hovering over your shoulder but people dropping by your workspace to say "hello" as they made their rounds to the breakroom or to their office. People were supportive and co-workers covered for each other. I remember one time a co-worker gave me brand-new bed sheets for my move and another ordered cupcakes just because she knew I liked them. When the weather was bad, they expected you to stay home, as a safety precaution, and we got paid for the day, regardless. I felt this was the ideal work environment; this was a team, comradery at its finest. Plus, I found it quite rewarding when I told people I worked for the top wedding source in the nation, which it was at the time.

As time went on, I decided to take on a part-time job to supplement my income. My grandmother had worked for this retail company and she was happy, so I decided to work retail on nights and weekends for some extra money and discounted clothes. How hard could it be? Plus, they paid more than my lovely full-time job at the wedding source. Little did I know the once welcoming environment at a department store, I will respectfully call *Watchmens*, would turn into a battlefield and I would learn a valuable lesson in how to stand my ground.

Standing your ground simply means to not ignore, waver, or back down from something you believe in, whether it's your morals, values, or company policy, regardless of what others may say or do to persuade you otherwise. It is putting your foot down, holding to your beliefs, being bold, and facing adversity, even when it's uncomfortable and unpopular. Remember the adage, "If you don't stand for something, you'll fall for anything"? In the subject of toxic environments, that quote has never been truer. In fact, if you don't stand up for what is right in this type of environment, you will be silenced, mistreated, disrespected, and disregarded, which could lead to a mountain of other issues.

With standing your ground in the workplace, I'm not encouraging you to pick a fight with everyone you feel has stepped on your toes, neither am I implying you walk around the office with a "Heck No, I won't go" sign for any issue where you have opposing beliefs. I am informing you to: 1) read and know your company policy; 2) be personally accountable for the information it contains; 3) expect others to also operate in its confines; 4) have moral standards and values; 5) don't voluntarily let someone corrupt, harm, or mistreat you; and 6) speak up when serious violations occur. Then once you speak up or out about a serious infraction, don't let someone intimidate you into silence. Advocate for what is right and if the violation is something less severe, just don't tolerate it. Learn how to walk away, talk it out, or just straight up ignore the foolishness and don't let it seep into your mindset and destroy your spirit. You cannot control others but you can control how you approach situations, people, and your reactions. It is all on you!

I know this firsthand from my experience with Watchmens. One of the things about being young or new to an established situation, is we may be afraid to speak up about something we know is wrong or that does not align with what we believe, in fear of being isolated or even fired. We don't want the negative attention it might bring, so we silence ourselves. If you silence yourself, it does not change the fact you are still miserable. In fact, the silence in this type of environment can be oppressive and physically and emotionally harmful as you internalize the negativity. It's also no secret that such silence will eventually affect your performance and cause you to have a disdain for your career in addition to seeping into other areas of your life.

Watchmens was my introduction of what it is like to be under a microscope because I was young, educated, and free (so I thought). I experienced discrimination and harassment at the hands of women who were older, uneducated, and stuck. You would think the struggles we have as women to succeed in a male dominant world, especially in managerial positions, there would have been, at least, some fairness but it was not the case.

The comradery among women or a sense of support for each other is not always a given in the workplace. There are situations where there is an unspoken sisterhood to naturally help each other succeed but sometimes there is also a discord called relational aggression, that seeks to cause social damage through intimidation, emotional abuse, and ostracizing tactics. Common among female co-workers, relational aggression can be viewed as "girls being girls" or diminished as a "cat-fight", when it is a serious workplace issue. An issue that causes emotional and psychological harm to victims due to power deviance in the aggressor. As a woman in my early 20's, I did not expect to experience this as a part-time sales associate at a national retail giant.

My first clue was at orientation. We sat in a conference room as the assistant store manager made it plain to us (six to ten new hires) that she worked 14 years in retail to earn her current position and it was because of longevity, unpleasantness to others, and hard work and not education. In her voiced opinion, she expressed how college graduates were privileged persons who labeled retail as easy and she would "dare" anyone with a degree to think they were better at her job than she, in which "they would have no chance at succeeding". We sat there in disbelief that someone in a managerial position would believe a pursuit of higher education was a negative thing. Little did I know, at that time, her statements were passive attempts to bully and intimidate, in the form of relational aggression.

The assistant manager was just the introduction to the forthcoming chaos; there was a store manager and women's department manager who would later surface to spread bitterness to all. I worked as a retail associate in the accessories department along with 10 ladies, six who were under the age of 30. We would often get surprise visits from the women's department manager, Christy the Creeper, who worked on the second floor but would somehow make her way down to the first floor, to our small department to see what we were doing. I gave her the pseudonym of the Creeper because she would literally creep around our department looking for any type of infractions so she could confront and report us; thus, her actions gave us the creeps. The word through the grapevine, the rumor in the store, was the Terror Squad (store manager, assistant store manager, and the Creeper) disliked our manager, Taj, because they felt he was lazy, privileged (he drove a sports BMW his father bought him), and "not strict" on his subordinates. Did I mention he also had a master's degree?

The Creeper hated our manager. I would overhear her conversations with one of the older women in my department about how Taj wasn't doing his job. I would admit, he was a bit of a flirt to some of the girls in the department. I saw him invite a few young ladies into his office to "discuss" but at least he kept the door open, just enough for us to peek and laugh like little school girls because we knew their "discussion" wasn't work related. Perhaps this is what perturbed the Creeper and inclined her to take watch over every young woman in the department because she surely never gave any of the ladies over the age of 40 any problems. In fact, she never said a word to them when she would come down on the first floor. She would bypass the 40+ ladies and come straight to the below 40 group and stare us down and make some unwarranted comment on how we could do our job better.

Two times stuck out in my mind and that was when I was closing a register early because we had two people left in the department to close out five registers within 30 minutes before closing and no customers waiting. In closing one of the registers, I accidently locked the keys inside. I called customer service so that a manager (as they were the only ones with register keys) could come unlock it. I should have waited for five minutes until 9pm to call but I did not and it resulted in a big strike against me. Who did they send to unlock the register? None other than the Creeper herself. Of course, I had to hear a lecture about how we are not supposed to close registers early. I explained that if the two of us closed all five registers at the call time, we would not be ready by 9:20pm, which is the expected time. She didn't care and this was a win-win situation for her because regardless, we were going to be in trouble. If only I hadn't locked the keys, they never would have known.

After she lectured me, she did the unthinkable. She.got.in.my.face. I was at the register which was in a circle, so she walked toward me as far as she could. As she got closer, I backed up until my butt was pressed against the counter and her nose was less than an inch from mine, so much so I had to turn my head to the right as not to get her breath on my lips. She said, in a forceful tone, "You better not close this register early ever again and if you do, I will find out and you will have to deal with me. Do you understand me?"

I was in shock because my own mother didn't even talk to me in that manner. I did not know what to do, I was so upset and uncomfortable. She hadn't instilled fear in me, if that was her intent, but her actions that night definitely angered me. Those angry feelings would resurface during my second encounter with her that would push me over the edge, which resulted in my filing harassment charges.

During the second encounter, my department co-workerAngela, and I were in the break room before our shift started. The store policy stated that employees working the last four hours of the day are allotted one 10-minute break at the beginning of the shift. We were doing that and as we were enjoying our last five minutes, the Creeper flings open the door and comes to our table (ignoring the other employees in the breakroom), pointing her finger in our faces and telling us "break time is over and no one should be in here." We explained and she told us if we didn't get up "instantly", she would write us up and then she left the room, never making a statement to the other three folks in the room. My co-worker finished her drink and left and I said, "No, when my five minutes are up, then I will leave."

Furious, I sent a letter, with the company's harassment policy attached, detailing the harassment directly to Watchmens' regional director because the store manager was the Creeper's friend and fellow member of the Terror Squad. Months later I was called into the store manager's office along with our new manager (they moved Taj to the daytime and promoted the Creeper's assistant manager as the night manager for my department). The store manager expressed her anger in my sending the letter to the regional director and not to her first. She tried to convince me that all of my complaints towards the Creeper were not harassment because harassment in the workplace is only acknowledged as sexual. I entertained her speech because I had to but I was empowered because I knew my rights and I knew the policy.

Most importantly, I knew what harassment (in this situation, some may call it bullying) was and felt I had done the right thing in standing up for myself; however, I was not oblivious to the target that was now placed on my back. Luckily for them, I had confidence in the company's retaliation policy.

The most disheartening thing was in the meeting I learned of her prejudices, ignorance of the company policies, and oppressive ways. I was bothered about how she tried to diminish my feelings and justify the Creeper's actions as "great supervision", desecrate my bachelor's degree because I was a mere clerk, and spotlight her work experience as a store manager as "better than an education". The baffling part is I never boasted about having a degree in orientation or at any time while working at Watchmens.. The reason some people knew I had a degree was because they asked me if I enrolled in college and I responded I had graduated. A degree of any kind is a major accomplishment but I never knew a bachelor's degree would be a scarlet letter. It was evident certain behaviors are a reflection of the organizational culture and such a culture is driven from the top. In a sense, the store manager was an oppressor.

The store manager not only spoke to me but she spoke with my co-worker, Angela, as well because I mentioned her name in the letter. Angela was angry with me because I used her name and she felt a target was now on her back too. Angela, a 19 year-old recent rural high school graduate, was more upset at the experience of being in the manager's office because she said it was intimidating, which made her cry, as did me. However, other department colleagues feltI did the right thing but were uneasy because they knew the entire department was now being watched.. Despite the mixed feelings, initially, the majority gave me kudos for my courage to stand up to the Creeper as others had also been harassed and because of my letter, no one in my department was harassed by the Creeper nor any other manager again.

In fact the Terror Squad did not even stop as much in the department anymore. Since our department was the pathway to the timeclock area, they would have to pass through but that is all they did. Every time they walked by, I did what my mother suggested. She was the one who encouraged me to write the letter. She told me if I didn't do anything to resolve the challenges I was experiencing, then I had no reason to complain and I needed to learn how to stand up for myself according to company policy and not lash out through anger with insults and confrontations. When the Terror Squad walked through, I made sure I acknowledged them and they made sure they spoke as well with a "Hello Porscha, how are you today?" And I would respond with a triumphant, "I'm fine and how are each of you ladies?"

The Lesson

The entire experience taught me a valuable lesson in the power of knowing the company policies and having the courage to stand up for what is right and for myself. We all have the right to work in an environment free of hostility and harassment, we don't have to be miserable. Perhaps, as I write this section, I realize this was the foundation for my advocacy for healthy work environments. It's funny how nothing is wasted in life and this possibly was the beginning of my journey to help others to thrive in toxic work environments.

What I experienced at Watchmens is nothing different than what a lot of people have experienced at the hands of work cliques and bullies. It is all driven by power and when you have a group like the Terror Squad, the clique collectively through their positions, enact control and oppress those who they deem as threats to who they are in their position. It's a survival instinct to prey on the weak or younger as to exercise authority and a lot of that is done through aggression. The power of control becomes stronger with the association or joining of forces with like minded folks to increase power and intimidate others as a facade to not attack.

What the Terror Squad was doing in every instance, was nothing short of intimidation fueled by relational aggression. From orientation to every time of working on the floor, it was clear power deficient was the driving force. Many times people choose to exercise their power through intimidation to make others feel less than, due to their own personal insecurities. Insulting one's personal accomplishments or differences from their own, is the type of mind games the Squad was playing in an effort to make others feel less than so they could feel better about themselves. I am sure many of you have encountered this type of common behavior on the job. It can be displayed in multiple ways and I know you could share some stories of your own, but regardless of the specific experience the action of it affects us the same.

It not only is abusive and oppressive, but leads to ostracism. If you make people scared to question you or challenge you whether right or wrong, then you have them under control to do what you will. Scholar Lutgen-Sandvick speaks of workplace bullying as a 'power-deficient' to where a person who wants to resign, decreases their work productivity and creates an uncomfortable experience even to those who are mere witnesses to bullying.

This was evident in how Angela, a victim of the Creeper, did not want to speak formally against it and was angry that I mentioned her name in the complaint, out of fear of the backlash and how she would be viewed by others in the department. I could only imagine the silencing tactics the store manager said to Angela in her meeting that would make her cry, to the point she did not want to discuss what was said. I'm sure it was nothing short of the store manager's attitude toward me of belittling my complaint by telling me my claims were invalid and were not heard by the executives. Essentially, her tactics to ostracize me were beyond what she said to me in her office. I would later find out she had informed the seasoned ladies in my department of my letter and my and Angela's meetings with her in an attempt to paint me as lashing out because I was caught shutting down the register before closing (my first encounter with the Creeper). Additionally, she had also asked them to encourage me to not pursue my claim any further, as it "might bring unwanted attention to the department", as said by one of my co-workers.

What I want you to take away from this experience is it is never okay for you to be mistreated on a job by anyone. If you tolerate it, then you have no one to blame. People will treat you anyway you let them. The workplace is always a sticky situation because it is your livelihood, if you don't work then you don't eat. That is why I want you to realize the power you have in oppressive situations. Your company policy can help you to understand not only the culture of your organization but use it to your advantage and your protection. In doing so, don't forget that it is a two-way street, so you are also held accountable to it as well. If you stick to the rules, then you always have support. Furthermore, if your company policy promotes inequalities and/or is absent of pertinent measures, seek change. When you start to blame others for your misfortune, you give them the power and then become dependent on them to set the mood for your life. I say "no", take control of your experiences. When you have to make tough decisions, then remember to stand your ground, it may take some time but the truth always prevails. Lastly, if the powers are unwilling to budge, then envision a workplace that is respectful for all and pursue it. Your health, peace, happiness, and state of mind are at stake...don't give it to them.

3 THE PSYCHOLOGICAL CIRCUS

I received a part-time job as an assistant that would forever change my life. *Upside down and inside out* would probably be the song lyrics most fitting for my eight year experience at what would be some of the best of times, the absolute worst of times, all the while being necessary times. Had it not been for my experiences there, I don't know where my professional career would have landed. It was there I was encouraged, supported, and introduced to my pursuit of a doctorate, given the opportunity to travel internationally, learned to play golf, met lifelong friends, and gained valuable professional experience and exposure. This organization took a chance on me when I had no other options and I am forever grateful.

This is also the place where I received the inspiration to write this book. Sure, I had experienced toxicity elsewhere, but never on this level. I started as a part-time assistant for the executive director and left as a director of communications, a former direct report for the senior vice president of the department. I saw people come and go and come and go again. I served on numerous committees and company-wide task forces and networked with several prominent executives in the city. With all I endured and accomplished, I was exposed to some unbelievable behaviors and personalities that provided many enlightening and jaw dropping experiences of which I will tell you about in various chapters of this book. I laughed, I cried, and at times shook my head in disbelief at some of the actions that took place. Honestly, it was too many to name and frankly, I forgot about some of them because they were just so ridiculous.

The best way to describe my experience in a nutshell, would be to call it what it was, a psychological circus. Many of you have worked in this type of toxic environment before, if not now. If you haven't, then maybe you are familiar with some of the psychological circus' main acts. The acts represent the personalities that keep the circus running. In short, difficult personalities are what keeps the work environment toxic. In this chapter we will discuss some of these main personalities as I offer ways to identify and handle them.

Personalities and Psychological Disorders

A toxic environment is not complete without the lovely people who have difficult personalities. It is important to understand that some personality traits, such as: stubborn, indecisive, and aloof can be difficult in certain situations but are easy triumphs in directing the benefits of the traits in the correct path. The personalities that are not just difficult but toxic are native to every toxic environment. The co-workers and managers who are rigid, aggressive, self-centered, passive-aggressive, and distrusting and/or who have dysfunctional behavior are the toxins you want to handle with care. Most of the time these personalities are based on psychological disorders (e.g. anxiety, paranoia, narcissism, and obsessive-compulsive disorder) that have manifested over a lifetime and some are caused by pivotal events that have altered an individual's workplace interactions. Regardless of the origin of the toxic personality, you have to be prepared to deal with all types of personalities on the job.

Taking responsibility for how you engage with them is the most effective tool. This means being able to recognize the traits of personality disorders and adjusting your way of work to accommodate the disorder complexities. I'm not saying you coddle or give passes for someone's behavior, but you should be proactive in taking a higher plane in your interactions. Sometimes you may not know you are dealing with a difficult personality until your interactions become challenging, uncomfortable, or weird. Should you find yourself in a situation with these characteristics, don't ignore your instinct; if you feel something was "off" after communicating with a coworker, believe it.

Personalities are indeed a reflection of a person's character. In the workplace, it is common for people to have a work persona outside of their normal, everyday personality as experienced with family, friends, and those persons unassociated with worklife. Just as people are able to act differently at work, it is important to separate one's behavior from who they are. What I mean is as you experience a colleague with a difficult personality, you must address the problematic behavior and not the actual person. For example, you don't say "Jesse is not a team player" but that "Jesse demonstrates a non-team player attitude because he chooses not to work with the team". 'Diane is not a backstabber but displays betrayal-like behavior because after agreeing with my disdain for our boss in a private conversation, she told him what I said in disagreement with my perspective.'

The key is not to label a person because of their behavior or for negative actions they have taken. Doing so categorizes them; thus, subjecting them to generalizations and stereotypical assumptions associated with prior experiences of people in that category. You cannot treat them based on who they are as a person because it would be a losing battle as you don't have the power or time to change a whole human being based on your work relationship. However, behaviors can be changed, altered, and managed. The trick is to interact with the toxins without taking in the toxicity; you want to thrive in these environments and not succumb to them.

Work Environment

Schneider (1984) in his classic article, *The people make the place*, explained the work environment as being one cultivated by people. The organizational structure, values, and culture are influenced by the attitudes, experiences, and behaviors observed by its employees. What this means is toxic environments are toxic, courtesy of the employees and their past and present experiences. Organizational processes are established based on the attitudes, feelings, and behaviors of the people. Therefore, organizations and work environments are fluid, metamorphosing to the customs of its people and attracting the talents of people to take it to its next level or help it maintain its identity. When understanding the work environment, you must consider its culture, which is typically established by its founders and perpetuated by its people and their personalities.

It is imperative to understand this for the simple fact the environment of your workplace is critical to your livelihood. Out of a day's 24 hours, approximately 12 are spent in preparation and traveling to work as well as actually working, for full-time 40 hour week positions. With half of your day spent in the workplace, the environment becomes a vital part of your life and what happens there has a significant effect on your identity, health, lifestyle, and personality.

Employees perform better in supportive work environments where they feel valued and where they have friends. It is the positive friendly relationships in the workplace that create a strong information exchange among employees, which organizations depend on for greater job significance, productivity, and performance. When things are the vast opposite, where environments are suppressive, lack allies, or no longer fit for our lives, our job performance decreases. As performance decreases, your career identity becomes questionable as your job is put in jeopardy because you no longer align or effectively contribute to the continuous cycle of the organization.

This is where you see that working on a job is more than just having a skillset to perform a series of tasks. When you interview, most of the time questions are not asked about how you will specifically perform the duties of the position. Primarily, the interview questions center on how you interact with people and how your personality is most aligned with the current employees. Job interviews boil down to how well you fit into the current environment. When you go through the appraisal process, it is how well you perform according to the organization's goals which is dictated by the organization's culture, again how well you fit.

Yes, the work environment is a complex entity on its own which takes various types of skill sets, personalities, and experiences to function. Whether you feel you actually fit into the organization or not, there is a particular uniqueness you bring to the table; so don't let anyone or any reason make you perform any less than your capabilities. Until things get better or until you find a greater opportunity (if that is what you want to do), you must know how to cope in your situation by taking a proactive stance when dealing with the difficult personalities.

My Experience

My encounters with difficult personalities came during my time as a budding professional at an historical organization, which as explained earlier, I likened to a circus. We had the senior vice president who was similar to a ringmaster. He was in control of the department (the show), provided direction and focus on the various acts in the show, participated in some of the top performances, and made declarations and sometimes hyperbolic excuses for the bizarre behaviors that were experienced. Clowns came in the form of entitled clients, ignorant colleagues, and random jerks. There were people who walked a tightrope in their job performance, focused on doing as little as possible while bending the rules as much as possible. Magicians who disappeared and reappeared asking for handouts, jobs, and favors, just when you thought you got rid of them years ago. Unicyclists who worked in silos, trapeze artists who bounced around and never settled on one job/task, trained animals, and jugglers. I quickly found myself juggling the various personalities and doing jobs the other performers discarded.

Working in the circus taught me some of the most valuable lessons of my life. I would not be the professional I am today and I would not have the tolerance and skill set had I not attended and participated in the circus for nearly a decade. I learned so much about people, the importance of looking at something from different sides of the spectrum, grassroots programming, and psychology all at the same time.

Psychological Disorders

As a member of the circus, my juggling act varied from tasks, projects, people, to personalities with my grand finale of an in-the-air combination at the end of each week. Many times the difficulty of my act came from the balancing of three major psychological disorders within the workplace. I'm sure there were more, but these are the ones that stick out. There were two forms of personality disorders in the form of odd behavior (paranoid) and erratic and overly dramatic behavior (narcissistic) and one anxiety disorder in the form of obsessive-compulsive disorder (OCD).

Paranoid personality disorder is described as pervasive distrust and suspiciousness of others such that motives are interpreted as malevolent. In essence, this is the "me against the world" person, who feels that everyone is out to get them. A trait of this personality disorder is this person suspects, without sufficient basis, that others are exploiting, harming, or deceiving them. They tend to read more into things than what was presented, written, or said. For instance, they take simple remarks or events as threatening or demeaning. They are prone to perceive their character or reputation is being attacked when it is apparent to others that it is not and their belief is others are always lying, cheating, or trying to harm them in some way. This becomes their reasoning for not wanting to work with others. I experienced this behavior in a colleague named Floral, who you will read about in a forthcoming chapter.

Narcissism came my way in the form of a former supervisor who I will call Medusa. The narcissistic is defined as a person having an inflated sense of their own importance and a deep need for admiration. These types have symptoms of being preoccupied with fantasies focused on unlimited power, beauty, love, intelligence or success. These folks have the tendency to exaggerate their own talents and achievements, while expecting to be praised and constantly admired. They devalue and exploit others and are self-centered, boastful, and arrogant, believing they are special and only understood by other special people. Specifically, they feel certain people are beneath them, so if you are not in a higher position than them or have any type of power that could potentially aid them, they would not consider you special. You must tread lightly with a narcissist because they have a hypersensitivity to insults, criticism, and defeat.

The final disorder I will address is obsessive-compulsive, which may be the lesser of the three disorders described; however, if they are paired with one of the other disorders, beware. OCD is the obsessive or intrusive irrational thoughts, ideas, or impulses that repeatedly well up in one's mind with compulsive or repetitive rituals. You know, that person who has to have everything on their desk facing the same way and has to walk in the door the same way each time, if not they feel obligated to enter five times until they get it right. Often they may have superstitions and insist on ritual actions that have no purpose except to relieve an obsession. You can identify this disorder in someone by their recurrent, persistent, intrusive, and excessive thoughts, impulses, or images. This person is more than likely perceived as 'weird' and not as toxic and destructive as the other two described disorders; however, when experienced, if unfamiliar with how to address them and deal with this disorder, you could be in for a rude awakening.

The list could probably continue about the various psychological disorders and as this book continues, you might discover some additional ones mentioned as you hear more about my career experience and the characters I mention. Again, I must reiterate, I am not diagnosing anyone, I'm just simply expressing my opinion based on my personal interactions with them as compared to literature about the mentioned disorders. From my experience, I have learned six helpful tips that have allowed me to cope and work well with the owners of these disorders.

When working with people with psychological disorders, you must first understand their affliction. Take time through reflective measures to process and think of constructive ways to deal with them. Don't go around interacting with this person as if they are thinking logically all the time and making sane decisions based on the work or task presented in front of them. Like I said, when you feel something is off, believe it. Monitor your emotional reactions and observe the effects of your actions with them. Make a mental note of how they handle certain constant situations and look for common trigger points that occur every time you notice the odd behavior. Then use the internet (from credible sources) for clarification of the traits you witnessed and seek understanding of what they are going through and look for reasoning of why they behave in such a manner. You don't have to do a full blown research paper on them. If you know when you walk into their office and touch something on their desk, every time they wipe it off or shift it back in place and get a little testy with you, then maybe that bothers them, so simply don't do it, no matter how minor it is. Remember, you are taking a proactive stance.

Always remember they are the one with the disorder and they live with this everyday, whereas you just have to tolerate it for a period of time whenever you have contact with them. Therefore, remain calm whenever you interact with them, as not to set them off or to argue. Keep in mind the old adage that *no one can distinguish the fool in an argument*. Besides, you want to be non-confrontational because your objective is to get what you need done from them or with them and get out. You will not succumb to the toxicity, so don't surround yourself or put yourself in the middle of toxic situations.

If you should find yourself having any concerns, besides the obvious, with them then remember to address them privately and frankly. Don't beat around the bush, don't try empty small talk because they will feel like you are setting them up for an attack and you want them to hear your undiluted message. You want to stick to the facts: A occurred and as a result B happened, and because of that it resulted in C and C is not beneficial. Leave what you thought or what someone said out the door. It only complicates the matter and then it allows them to bring their feelings and their point of view, which is heavily influenced by their disorder into play and you won't win because it will be a comparison of apples and oranges and the solution won't come without havoc. You want to keep them at ease.

It is important to also give them specific and immediate feedback. If they did something wrong, let them know what they did wrong and why it was wrong as soon as you can in a safe environment. A mistake would be to wait several months until they have done something several times before you bring it up to them. If they offended you, say it when the offense happens; however, do this in a calm and private conversation. You never want to respond to them in a negative light with others around. It will go wrong fast and it will only strain the relationship even more.

For example, you could say "Marlon, when you get a chance, can I run something by you quickly?" Then in a private environment, you would give them feedback. Begin with an affirmative, provide the specific setting for the situation, state the fact of what happened and the result. Allow them a chance to respond to a specific question, as there could be a valid reason or a different perspective you were unaware. Then follow-up with feedback and consequence. "Thank you for giving me a couple of minutes of your time. Yesterday when we were in the staff meeting, I noticed you did not have the part of your presentation complete with the sales numbers as agreed upon in our team meeting. Not having those numbers made us, as a team, seem unprepared to provide the forecast for the next fiscal year. From your perspective, what prevented the numbers from being included on the slide? Going forward, if there is information you know is missing, please let the team know so that we can work together to get the correct information. When this happens, we all win as a team and no one is singled out."

You want to always remain positive when interacting with them. Though you may be amidst a negative situation, remaining positive helps to prevent further altercations and regrets in what you may say or do in the heat of the moment. No matter how much effort they may put in trying to drag you to their level, aim high so you remain professional in the situation because you never know who is watching. Remember you are the sane one. Always respond in a positive way and if you feel you cannot, announce your departure from the conversation and walk away quickly to regroup. You may have to take a break, go to your car and yell, or even go home for the day, but you must not lose your cool. Your reputation is at stake and you should never let anyone have the power over you to make you do something you know is not right or appropriate.

Lastly, don't ever, ever, ever, tell them they have a disorder. Do not tell them their behavior is like a disorder. This is confrontational, insulting, and demeaning, and an irrelevant point to share with these people. They will naturally defend themselves and this could lead to human resource troubles and overall communication and interaction barriers for you as this defeats the purpose of thriving in the toxic environment. Telling them and setting them off to release the effects of their disorder in the environment only contributes to the toxicity. Again, you must not succumb to the environment but learn how to thrive in it. Yes, it literally is a psychological circus.

Psychology in the Workplace and Documentation

When you begin to experience discomfort on your job or when your performance appraisal rating starts to decrease, it normally is an indication due to the effect of some aspect rooted in psychology. Whether it's a result of

Maslow's hierarchy of needs theory not being met, external factors affecting how you perceive your job, how you feel about co-workers or vice versa, how you feel about the role of your job, it all is based on behaviors and your perception of how and what the job or organization means to you and your desired lifestyle. It is all psychology.

Understanding the role of psychology in the workplace, especially in the area of psychological disorders, taught me how to deal with difficult people. I learned the hard way about the science of documentation, which in toxic work environments, will be a lifesaver. It helps to keep the facts and builds a case, if you should ever have to show proof, which you will if you have to make a claim. The saying goes, "it's always two sides of the story and then there's the truth". I have found when it is someone's word against yours, the truth is what you can physically produce, hence documentation. There is also another well known saying, *If you didn't document it, it never happened.* Even in contract disputes, it is what is on paper that counts, not what was said verbally. Will it be time-consuming...absolutely, but if you do it as you go, it won't be half as daunting as trying to remember what happened, who was there, and then trying to search for emails. Plus, when dealing with disorders, you may have to approach them and giving them specific feedback will be a key in your communication. Use your brain, you know when something is not right.

Documentation is taking notes in a meeting and then filing it where you can easily find it. Remember to keep your files organized and secure. People will get paranoid and nosy, seeing you record everything; I wouldn't put it past anyone to randomly go through your things "looking for something". I say this because I have caught people browsing in my file cabinet for something they were to get off my desk. I know people who make notes in a journal they take with them throughout the day. You could easily take notes via an electronic device as your phone, tablet, and laptop, just ensure your notes are backed up and accessible for you outside of the work environment. I've seen others who have very organized email folders where they file important emails received and sent. I've also noticed the use of a recorder on their phone or some type of recording device to flat out record meetings, conspicuously and inconspicuously, including video.

I would suggest finding what works best for you in your specific environment. I used a combination of taking notes and filing them away in folders with their names on it (code names of course, in case they went on a search in my office) and saving emails. With the emails, as soon as I received a foul one, I would print it out and file it under their name and also forward it to my personal email address. When strange things occurred, I immediately would go to my office and document it with the date, time, and parties involved.

My lesson on documentation came when I found out my supervisor at The Circus, who had narcissistic behavior patterns, was a habitual liar and master manipulator, two major deficits and identifiers of toxic leadership. It was at a time when I was working in the administration office of the senior vice president (The Ringmaster) under the supervision of the director of public relations. My supervisor, who I refer to as Medusa because she was a physically beautiful woman, who on the surface seemed nice but once you got to know her, you realized how much of a monster she was and how much rage she possessed, much like the Greek myth. Her capacity to lie in your face and behind your back, selfish ambition, and ruthlessness is what made her a monster.

I witnessed first hand how she used people to get what she wanted and intentionally befriended people for malicious intent just to toss them aside, with no remorse after she got what she wanted. Most did not see it coming because of her beauty: she had high cheekbones, slanted eyes, and bronzed skin. Her hair was long, dark, and curly and she had a nice feminine curvy silhouette. However, her lies were like serpents and if you looked at her hard enough, if you fell for her facade because of her looks, yes, it was like turning into stone. In the perspective of a circus, she would be like a snake charmer, performing dangerous acts by hypnotizing disarmed snakes to follow her commands as she sits outside of striking distance.

I had worked on a part-time basis for the office under Medusa and with that, had little interaction with her. The receptionist at the front desk hated her but I never knew why and never really inquired because I thought my time in the office was only for a short period, so I just did my work and left each day. It was just a job to get me through my graduate program but after not getting my dream job in the sports and entertainment industry, it became my reality.

In fact, it was my first full-time job as an entry level marketing specialist. Most would have been excited about having this job created for them but it just was not what I imagined. I am not sure if I was blinded by my own ambition, thinking that graduating with my master's degree would somehow solidify my place as a "professional". The visions of well-dressed, no nonsense women leading in the boardroom on television, magazines celebrating the corporate success of women in male-dominated positions, and propaganda of how a graduate degree was this golden ticket that somehow thrusts you into a senior leadership position all filled my head, made my chest poke out a little further, and gave me hope that I was well on my way to executive stardom.

When I began as a college freshman I selected pre-business because I could see myself in a business suit (literally this is the only reason, otherwise my major would have been undecided). This black blazer and skirt suit was fitted to show my shape yet professional enough to command respect and my white blouse with the crisp collar and gold necklace whispered femininity while my 4-inch black pumps confirmed my intelligence. Yes, I rehearsed my walk in this suit several times as I stood to make presentations in front of clients who clapped at the end of my marketing pitches, received standing ovations at conventions where I was the keynote speaker, and twirled in my back massaging chair in my luxurious office overlooking the New York skyline. I was a six-figure gal managing a productive staff, making executive decisions, driving a luxury car, smooshing with the rich and famous, and enjoying the finer things in life thanks to my hard work, determination, and education. But ladies and gentlemen, just like Dr. Martin Luther King Jr. at the Washington Monument, Christopher Wallace on the steps of a Brooklyn brownstone...it was all a dream.

No one bothered to wake me up from this dream. In fact society constructed it, the education system fueled it, companies sold it, and I bought it. I graduated from college and the next year entered graduate school, just to receive only one offer as a marketing specialist making a mere $35,000 a year. I was hopeful because the job was created for me with the promise to move up once I gained solid experience. And that it did, but it was a rollercoaster on the way.

The senior vice president's office was a suite that contained his office and Medusa's office in the back and in the front was my office and the receptionist desk. Everything was fine at first, our interactions were professional, initially, until Medusa decided she needed to keep tabs on what I was doing throughout the day. That was understandable and I met with her faithfully every Monday morning at 9 am. It started off legitimate, she would ask me what I was working on for the week, give me assignments and deadlines, and that was it. I started taking notes to write down my given assignments not knowing they would later serve as a record of what she told me to do when she would claim differently.

Overtime, the morning meetings became bitch sessions, where she began to talk about The Ringmaster (senior vice president) and her disdain for some of the things he was doing and how she was undermining his efforts. She also started speaking negatively about others in our building in regards to their, from her perspective, lack of intelligence and physical looks, mental capacity, and personal issues. It was at that time, red flags went off because a person in a managerial position should not be discussing things of this matter with a subordinate. I began to think, 'if she talks about others in front of me, then she will do the same to me'. I learned to only discuss things related to business, never share my personal feelings about someone with her, not get caught up in the gossip, and write down what she communicates to me. Here is when I began to understand her two-faces and measured what she said to how she acted and found plenty of disparities. I then began to dread our weekly meetings because it was no longer about the job but about gossip.

It became extremely taxing to deal with her but it was a necessary task as her direct report. You know someone lies too much when your supervisor's boss (The Ringmaster) tells you they don't trust your supervisor because your supervisor lies and has lied about them, so they know they have lied about you. I had known she was a liar because at first her lies were behind my back but when she started lying in my presence, yes lying on me in my presence to The Ringmaster, then that's when it had gotten too far and my receipts (documentation from our meetings) came in handy.

My first instance I had documented of her lies was when she had sent an email to me and the receptionist, Jaime, with high priority, chastising us about a submitted report that didn't get The Ringmaster's approval. She stated verbatim with no salutation, "Send [The Ringmaster] a copy of the Thursday Report you submitted on Feb 5 ASAP. He was not pleased to find out that you submitted it without his review or approval. Both of you should know that everything that is sent from this office must be reviewed by him. There is no excuse for not sending him a copy to look over, especially since he was in the office that day. I urge both of you to be more mindful of proper protocol in the future."

I was caught by surprise, though I should not have been but it was the first time I was experiencing one of her lies directly. I immediately thought, *Excuse me! I don't even know what report you are talking about and because I don't do any reports on behalf of the senior VP, why am I even receiving this email?* That's when I knew something was up. She copied The Ringmaster on this, so now he thinks I sent a report that I didn't even know existed without his approval. I hadn't worked with the receptionist on any projects, so how did I get involved in this situation?

During our daily meeting, I expressed to her that I was upset she would accuse me of sending a report I had no knowledge of and then copy The Ringmaster on it. She to my face says that it was meant for Jaime but the senior vp had thought I was helping with the report. *So when does helping someone with a report constitute sending a report?* It doesn't. Jaime did not report to me, she reported to Medusa just like I did, so how could I even get mixed up in this unless something else occurred that I wasn't aware of. Medusa then tells me she would notify The Ringmaster that I had nothing to do with the report. My thoughts were, *as my supervisor, this was common knowledge that I didn't complete that report and you should've said that to him before even sending the email to me, right?* Right! It was at that point, I was assured she was sneaky and untrustworthy.

Additionally, there had been countless times The Ringmaster would assign her work and she would give it to me to do in addition to my actual work and then take credit for it. Meanwhile, she would tell me her responsibilities had priority over my work and when I was late getting my work done, because she told me to do her work at the last minute, she would tell me to "do better", while at the same time telling The Ringmaster that I was 'falling behind on my work'. I was familiar with delegation of responsibilities at that time in my life and knew managers were infamous for taking credit for the work of their subordinates. However, to audaciously give all your work to your subordinate and then make negative comments about their speed of performance is demented.

A novice, I worked harder and faster to get both of our tasks done. Meanwhile, she spent her time on the phone with her so-called boyfriend. When I caught on to what she was doing, I would never tell her my progress with her work and would give her the finished product in front of The Ringmaster to let him know it was me who completed the work. I knew he had to figure out what was happening because at that time, I wasn't as good of a writer as she. Medusa had become so lazy that she stopped correcting my mistakes on her work before she submitted it.

Previous times she would give me a deadline and it was a couple of days before she had to submit to him, which would give her time to review and revise before their meeting. Apparently she had stopped proofing it and he was catching the mistakes. In the meetings, she would have some lame excuse about how she missed the mistakes and tell The Ringmaster he was giving her too much work to do in a small amount of time. Then she would look at me to support her claim of being overworked. I'd just sit there with a blank stare. *Seriously! You're looking at me for back up when you do nothing?!* The next morning, she had the audacity to reprimand me because The Ringmaster caught the mistakes on her work.

I was absolutely fed up and frustrated because I had no one I felt I could confide in. I took matters into my own hands and not only did I hold her work until the meetings with The Ringmaster, I said "Hey Medusa, here is the work you had me do." When he would ask her a question about the progress, she would look at me for help but I would just sit there with a blank stare. Sometimes I would speak up on the progress but when I did so I would say, "I checked on it yesterday and found...." as a passive note to let him know I actually did the work.. He eventually caught on and then started calling me into his office to confirm things and one day flat out asked me about the amount of her work I was completing.

With documentation in hand, I told him everything. Then he proceeded to tell me how she continuously made the complaint that I did not complete my work. Appalled, but since I had his ear, I asked about the whole Thursday Report fiasco. He informed me the sending of the report wasn't the big deal Medusa had made it out to be and in fact, Medusa had told him I made Jaime send it but when Jamie expressed her disdain of Medusa's email, she (Jaime) admitted I never had anything to do with the report or its sending.

This was a long story of many to demonstrate the foundation of the toxicity I would experience in this environment. It is because of this scenario, The Ringmaster would eventually remove her as my supervisor to be his direct report. I used the word "eventually" because The Ringmaster would have to hear a few more from her web of lies and experience her not doing what she was supposed to do until he reached his breaking point and publicly stripped her of office management duties and gave them to me.

This new management position was a gift and a curse. As office manager, my workload increased again because I was doing minor aspects of his job. At least this time, he acknowledged the work I did for him and didn't lie, but he gave me a lot of work to do. I did the work and it made Medusa furious because he used me as a pawn to get back at her. He would give her something to do and she would take awhile to complete it; frustrated he had yet to receive it, antagonistically he'd say, "I'll just give it to Jackson, at least I know it will get done."

Of course Medusa hated every moment of this missile launch. I quickly found myself in the middle of a silly battle; though it was a new thorn in my side, it gave me great experience in problem-solving. With the mention of my name, Medusa would bad mouth me and insult my abilities, especially my writing (she was a better writer, no one argued with that). The Ringmaster would then rebuttal with "I'd rather go with someone who does it than someone who doesn't". He praised her on her writing ability while in the same sentence noting others who were better writers, daggered with how her writing skills were the only thing she could do better than me. I was flattered and watchful when I walked to my car all at the same time. In their quarrels, he would be known to mention that I worked at a faster pace, was more detail-oriented, accurate, educated, and pleasant to work with.

Furious at the constant comparison between us and with me being on the favored end of that comparison, she would then seek to make me her competition and look for every opportunity to throw me under the bus, make my work life horrible, and turn people against me. Especially people who were new to the office, she conjured up stories about how I was under The Ringmaster's 'spell' and couldn't be trusted because I was "sneaky". All the while she was actually describing herself. The new folks believed this snake charmer because she was extremely welcoming to them by extending lunch invites where she'd pay the tab and engaging in personal conversations with them. You could say she might have had success as a politician because she ran a successful campaign. It worked because I'm the direct opposite, I don't talk to you unless it is about the job and getting work done, so it appeared what she said was true because I kept to myself and I was always in The Ringmaster's office because he was always assigning me tasks. This is a clear example of the power of perception.

Furthermore, Medusa stooped to sabotaging the works and comradery in the office. She continued to build relationships with the staff in the office, who she cared less about, inside and outside of the office under the pretense she could help them professionally. In return, they confided in her and she told their intimate personal details and laughed at their misfortune all behind their backs. She also conspired against them when they disagreed with her or was not of use to her in a particular situation. Medusa even went as far as to ruin the trust and respect the office staff had of The Ringmaster by encouraging them to demand salary raises, complain about their workloads, and strike against parts of the job they did not want to do and the worst part, she convinced them to do this directly to his face. Given their talent, ability, and the demeanor in which they approached him about these things, resulted in insubordination reprimands and demotions. When they came to complain to her about what happened as a result of her advice, she denied telling them to do that. It was at that time they would come to me for help.

Medusa was divisive, especially when she didn't get her way. No one in that office meant anything to her. She continued to create chaos in the office with the intent to reclaim her position as office manager. She did her best to prove I could not handle it. She even went as far as to give my assistants work to do and telling them it took precedence over the work I had assigned them. It was hell.

The ultimate example of deceit was when she was the chair of the organization's annual scholarship gala. Somehow she convinced The Ringmaster to let her hire an event planner because she didn't have enough help to pull it off. At this point she understood no one in the office trusted her and frankly, she said no one was talented enough to help her with the gala. This is narcissistic behavior at its finest, devaluing others and thinking only special people, such as her, can plan this event.

To make a long story short, The Ringmaster ended up having me attend the meetings with her and the event planner when deadlines were being missed. In doing so, I noticed during each meeting, she would complain to the event planner about how no one was on her level; she was so much better than others in the office because she was in a different social circle and that is why she had hired the planner. I quickly realized the planner had not done anything because Medusa hadn't given her any directives. Stunned, I soon got a tip from someone in the office that overheard one of her conversations about planning a trip to Switzerland with a gentleman friend the same week of the gala and that is why she had been dragging her feet on meeting the deadlines. She had no intention of being there and was not going to tell anyone. She wanted to prove things would fall apart if she wasn't present.

There are many other examples about her behavior that created a toxic work environment. The documentation I had on her, which included notes from our Monday morning meetings, the complaints from others in the office, my personal notes of her behaviors in meetings, interactions, emails, and such, all proved to help in the ultimate reprimand The Ringmaster gave her that calmed her down for a few months and led her to search for a new job.

The documentation also helped me to deal with her and rise above the toxins she spewed. I figured out how to use reverse psychology in stroking her ego to get her to complete work. I learned how to reward others in the office for doing the work I had given them, as to diminish the value of Medusa's requests, and how to get things done without involving her at all. With the documentation, I would go to her office and let her know the specific date and time she had given my assistants work and explain how it was a violation according to the process of going through me first to give them tasks. I would explain to her the benefits of the process for the entire flow of the office as a way to demonstrate my authority as office manager.

In his study of toxic managers, Roy Lubit (2004) described four different types: grandiose psychodynamic, grandiose learned, control freak, and antisocial. Despite the type, the author suggests seeking mentorship as the key and lists: showing admiration, avoiding criticism, seeking allies, avoiding provocation, and documenting your work as specific ways to handle each type of narcissist colleague.

Having a manager who exhibits this behavioral disorder, you could experience their ruthlessness, aggression, and destructive ways at any given time. The result is low morale, work diversion, and an interference in the organizational information exchange, which is significant to job performance and satisfaction. Toxic managers complicate the work environment and have the potential to destroy your career. Therefore, learn to quickly understand the underlying factors for the particular manager's behavior, recognizing lack of self-love, fear, and insecurity as common symptoms, and take heed to Lubit's suggestions as to put yourself in the best position of protection from their wrath.

My mistake with dealing with Medusa was I would not exercise my power as manager and would not say how what she did affected me. Holding things in only added to the animosity I had with her and it suppressed me. However, once I realized The Ringmaster had set me free from being under her rule and once I realized her narcissistic ways, I was able to claim the power in my position and find ways to work with her and around her in order to get the job done. Sure the environment still had its toxic ways but at least I was no longer suffering from the venom she was releasing and I was thriving as office manager, despite the environmental toxins.

4   CLIQUES, TRICKS, & FRIENDSHIPS

Birds of a feather flock together has been a colloquialism to explain that our identity is defined by people with whom we associate. Similar goals, characteristics, upbringings, and interests, are some of the areas that bond us to feed our sense of belonging. What it all equates to is understanding we are all connected in this world. Searching to belong is a basic human need psychologists deem as being on the same level as the desire for food and shelter. It is a necessity that helps us to create value in our lives, which is built on our common experience. Whether we are on teams, at social events, church, service projects or with family, we are consciously and subconsciously sizing up people and sparking conversations to identify a connection, an element of belonging to something greater than ourselves.

In the workplace, our search for belonging is no exception. People derive their identity from the social connections made from their employment. We find support, information, motivation, and happiness through the development of workplace relationships, which can take place in the form of friendships, cliques, associations, and alliances. Workplace friendships are critical in having a healthy and supportive working environment. Such positive relationships increase productivity and intrinsic motivation along with promoting job significance among employees. Furthermore, workplace friendships create a social network within the company that promotes communication and interaction. Think about it, you are more likely to share information with someone you like, will work better as a team, be more considerate and understanding, and assist them with a project because you have a positive relationship. You have someone to go out to lunch with, someone to vent to, and someone to ask questions. Researcher C. Dickie (2009) found work friendships help maintain organizational goals, promote innovativeness and supportive behavior, increase the sharing of work experiences, and help in breaking stereotypes and glass ceilings.

Yes, working in a friendly work environment is ideal for both the organization and its employees. The benefits are less stress, increased productivity, promotion, support, and friendship. Who wouldn't want a positive and nurturing environment? The reality is some of us will experience the opposite. Just as friendships have positive effects on the work environment, they can also lead to negative actions, such as: isolation, bullying, gossiping, ostracizing, rumors, shunning, and cliques. You may have guessed it, these factors contribute to a toxic work environment.

Toxic work environments cannot be perpetuated by one person, it takes a group. This is where those birds of a feather begin to mount up. Toxic environments are full of work relationships fueled by nepotism, favoritism, gossip, loyalty displacement, and office politics. The factors are the ammunition to turnover, harassment, dependence, low productivity, reduced loyalty, and straight up chaos.

Whether you stay and are satisfied with an organization relies heavily on your level of job embeddedness. Job embeddedness is what we talked about in a previous chapter, which is your fit within the organization. How you link with other people, how you interact with others in teams and groups, departments, and how you perceive your fit within those aspects. Basically, your level of job embeddedness is a predictor of turnover due to the intent to leave based on one's perceived fit into the organization. In other words, if during your search you don't find the birds of your feather with whom you can connect to share your experiences, vent, exchange information, and gain support, then the probability of you leaving the organization is high and the probability of you being unhappy is extremely high. When you have organizations where there is no attention focused on job embeddedness, it leans to foster an environment with toxicity.

Allies and Management

When I started working at The Circus I could care less about having a friend there. I was perfectly fine with my part-time schedule where I would keep the conversations to a minimum, do my job, and leave. However, when I decided to begin a career and seek full-time employment and promotion, I quickly learned my silo would be a recipe for disaster. Remember, a sense of belonging is desired by everyone and because I didn't search for it at that time doesn't mean others weren't searching for it with me. In fact, sometimes when you work in a silo in the vein to stay out of office politics, you can unknowingly isolate yourself. You have to learn to walk a fine line of being social to succeed. As stated before, it's all about the fit in an organization and that doesn't exist just at the interview but for your duration in the organization.

Being naturally shy, I have learned how to keep to myself while sharing just enough to communicate. You need allies, people who will speak to your character and join in an effort with you. You may not have regular conversations or know much about them but just saying 'hello' in the hallway and showing common courtesy can go a long way, especially if you need something done. Your continuous pleasantries can result in just the help or source of information you may need in difficult times. You need associations, people who you associate with maybe from working on a project together. You may not have a relationship with them but you have interacted positively with them and maybe an occasional quick conversation. They may not share much information with you but you know them well enough to vouch for their work ethic and they for you.

What we discuss in this chapter are the friendships and cliques that take place in the work environment. They can be good for those in it and bad for those outside of it. I can confirm I had a work friendship that derived from the toxicity and we are still friends to this day, though neither of us still work there. We were able to vent to each other, give each other a heads up when an issue was to arise with the other, and we had each other's back when one of us was being challenged. It made a world of difference because I felt like I had support and I wasn't in the toxicity alone. Had I not had her friendship, I might have broken down or broken someone else down, which either way means I probably would have been unemployed.

After working a year in what would be my first full-time job, I was excited about the opportunity to become a manager. Receiving this promotion this early was a huge step in my career and it was a privilege to now be the office manager. In this new position, I had high hopes of motivating others, bringing organization to the fold, and growing as a leader. I was young, the highest educated person in the office (after The Ringmaster), hard-working, and eager to take on new challenges to give me experience. I was ready!...or so I thought. Have you ever heard of the saying, "there's a *sucka* born every minute"? Well, hello my name is Porscha and at that point in time, I was the *sucka*. I didn't even get a raise or any incentive for taking this position, what I would soon find out would be a burden.

It happened on a whim. The Ringmaster called me into the office praising me for my work and how as a new graduate, managing the office was a great opportunity to have managerial experience on my resume… yahta, yahta, yahta. I drank the Kool-Aid. In the end, I found out it had nothing to do with my work but everything to do with my naivety. The truth was, I was a young woman in the South with a MBA and no real job offers but who had drive and talent without on-paper experience. I was desperate for a chance to gain experience and so I was handed what would be the start of my involvement in dealing with insanity, face to face.

So here I am, handed the office manager job in an office meeting after The Ringmaster hostilely stripped it from my supervisor because of what he would describe in the staff meeting as "her childish behavior". I am getting my first promotion in a little less than a year on the job in front of all of the professionally older department staff and on the heels of a public disciplinary action against my direct supervisor, Medusa. Needless to say, this did not go over well, especially because this was Medusa's first time hearing this news.

In total shock I could not say "no", although at times I wished I had enough guts and foresight to have bowed out gracefully. In the vein of progress and with gratitude, I became the proud new owner of an office of dysfunction, inheriting backbiting, manipulation, insubordination, and a crew of personalities that would incarcerate my happiness. I was now the supervisor to: an overpaid non-traditional intern who I will refer to as Emmy the Squatter, because she tried and succeeded at manipulating pretty much everything as you will find out later; Blockhead, the part-time payroll clerk with a "you can't tell me what to do" attitude; and two of the most innocent and impeccably smart traditional interns a manager could ever want.

When the offer to become manager of the office became my dangling carrot, I worked harder to show myself worthy of the position. I believed becoming a manager was the key to achieving my dream and therefore perceived it as hopeful. I received (after working the position for a few months) a bump in salary. I was happy because I pursued it and asked for it but as the saying goes 'be careful what you ask for…'. In hindsight the pay increase was not worth the agony I would have to endure. Sure it gave me experience and a mountain of stories to laugh at…NOW…but *wasn't nothing funny* when I was going through those years.

Receptionist Blues

One of my first lessons in management was 'more responsibility, more problems' which includes understanding that those who once were your 'friends' may have a hard time accepting you in your new role, especially as their manager. I learned quickly to not believe all the congratulatory remarks, as some were fueled by jealousy. Humans tend to put people in categories and sometimes boxes. Once you get outside of the box they put you in, it's like pieces of hell breaking loose. They may be happy for you when you are promoted over someone else, but when the promotion is over them, prepare for a rude awakening. I had to start by saying 'goodbye' to lunch invites and 'hello' to cold shoulders.

Among this new breath of management air, I had to endure the blues of managing a merry go round of receptionists for the front desk. We had no budget to hire someone full-time, so The Ringmaster had the brilliant idea of hiring interns or young graduates, in order to save money. This idea brought a multitude of superfluous drama and toxicity. There were two memorable receptionists who literally gave me the blues.

The Squatter

What would the office be without the drama? I'm sure we've all asked this question a time or two, whether we were in the drama or not, but you can't have drama without its king or queen. Suzanne Degges-White (2017) actually discusses the Drama Queen personality disorder. The author describes it as someone who, in the beginning, seems to be an engaging and pleasing employee but their melodramatics result in office chaos from their overacting and demand of attention at any cost. Well, this section is about a specific type of drama queen, who will go by the name of Emmy because after her weekly performances on the job, she definitely deserved one.

A beautiful woman with a soothing voice and a helpful attitude. A wife and new mother, who was seeking a full-time job while continuing her education. To my boss, she seemed like the perfect public face and fit to be the receptionist for his office. Emmy was poised to bring a mature yet delightful presence to all office visitors. She was pleasant and patient when answering the office phone and directing guests and visitors; she was assertive when trainers and staff tried to barge their way into his office; she had the basic technology skills to complete simple reports and keep his calendar; and she had the ability to set-up conference rooms and organize documents in preparation for his meetings. The girl even ensured The Ringmaster had water and coffee and independently called persons he was meeting with to ensure they were showing up on time to the meetings. As the office manager, this was the solace we needed in the office after having a few mishaps with previous receptionists.

In about a month, things began to slowly unravel. After five months, it was clear she had gone from being a solution to being a problem. Emmy was not the mature budding professional we deemed her to be but in fact was a seasoned con artist and professional liar who had auditioned for a receptionist job in order to receive a paycheck in exchange for her drama.

As the office manager, I had to bear the brunt of this hire (which I did not have any hand in hiring or selecting). The challenges with Emmy was she took a lot of time off, didn't complete her work, made excessive mistakes, altered her hours, created division in the office, and played the victim each time someone called her on her plot. The characteristics of Emmy are not unique to her as a person but indeed a type of employee that exists everywhere.

Managing this worker requires thoroughness in communication because they are always looking for a loophole. In the circus, her ability to conform into different roles to lie her way into sacred spaces can be likened to a contortionist. It's similar to a squatter, they occupy a space in hopes to reap the benefits instead of utilizing their time to secure a stable situation for themselves. If you make the slightest mistake or give them an inch, they'll use it to their advantage but against you. If you work with this type of person, you simply have to watch your back because working on a team with them means they won't pull their weight. Any information, resourceful or damning, they'll use to their advantage in an effort to make themselves appear favorable.

The Squatter is notorious for masquerading as a model employee. In the beginning everyone likes them because they do and say all the right things. They are a breath of fresh air. They are caring, intuitive, helpful, and friendly. However, it's a performance and the show does not last because they cannot sustain the act for too long as their true intentions slowly emerge. The reality is they will do just enough to maintain what they think is expected of them until they can find their next gig or squeeze themselves into another situation. In a nutshell, contortionists are squatters and squatters are opportunists.

Trick #1: Find an ally to cover for you

It was clear Emmy saw a promising opportunity in working in our office. She had heard about our challenges in finding a reliable receptionist and quickly saw a window to earn an easy paycheck. She was correct; however, her cunningness had company she wasn't prepared to compete against. Emmy had become instant friends with Blockhead, connecting over the struggle of balancing motherhood, college, and marriage. They covered for each other in the office, so the other could take care of their personal business on company time. The two would form an alliance against the rest of the office until the cunningness in both would naturally meet head on with a battle for domination. In one corner we had Emmy, a budding con artist from the Heartland of America. In the other corner, it was Bobbi Blockhead, a sassy, spoiled, slick employee from the mean East Coast streets, who like the human blockheads of the circus creates an illusion of toughness through acts of driving things into their skulls. It was ultimately a territorial showdown in which longevity prevailed.

After a huge disagreement with Emmy, I conveniently received a tip from Bobbi Blockhead that Emmy had submitted her timesheet falsifying hours worked. In fact the hours in question were times Bobbi had to fill in as receptionist, something she hated doing and was doing more often as the two grew closer. As the smoke cleared, Bobbi slowly realized she had been conned, as there was no reciprocity in their alliance...the irony. When I spoke to Emmy about the timesheet, she immediately ran to The Ringmaster to arrange a deal to work after office hours to make up the time. Why he would even agree to such a thing baffled me as once the office closes, there was nothing for her to do. When I spoke to him about it, he explained that he hadn't approved it; thus, she insisted he had reneged on what he said.

Trick #2: Lies & Disappearing Acts

Emmy's issue of falsifying hours was taken to another level once she was exposed by her former ally. She had moved on to no call/no show. Once called on it, she began to give written last minute notices of her absence or tardiness. The moment this became excessive and when she realized she wasn't getting paid for hours she did not work, she began to produce false doctor's notes. For some reason, she thought a doctor's note entitled her to get paid without having to work. Next, she would show up for work and leave for hours at a time, stating she had an intern employee resource group (ERG) meeting. Sometimes, she would say "I'll be right back" and would in fact go across the street to her home for a couple of hours. It baffled me that as an hourly receptionist, she thought she would get paid for lunches and doctor's appointments.

After all of these antics, plus many more not shared in this book, Emmy had moved from alliance to isolation, after burning everyone in the office with her lies and deception. The office staff and staff outside of our office were aware of her antics and some decided to conduct their own investigations. These investigations were of course a service to themselves because every time Emmy was away from her desk, it meant someone else in the office had to fill in for her, which was an inconvenience.

In their investigation, some went as far as attending Emmy's ERG meetings to see if she was there and to document the start and end times of her meetings. I remember they brought back proof (via a note on the door saying the meeting was canceled) demonstrating she wasn't at the meeting but yet left her desk. This led to one of the biggest blowups in the office which caused her to file a letter of harassment and defamation of character and spawned two shouting matches and physical threats among three employees in the office.

I remember this encounter all too well. While I was gone to lunch, Emmy went to her ERG meeting and was supposed to go to lunch immediately afterwards. Before she left, she told Medusa so she could cover the front desk in her absence; however, Medusa and Miss B were a bit perturbed because they had planned to take lunch together at the time Emmy left.

When I returned to the office, I was immediately pulled into Medusa's office with Miss B and the door shut as they vented about their displeasure with Emmy. They stated she was a liar because they had proof she had not gone to her ERG meeting and was now ruining their lunch plans. In the midst of Miss B's loud rant, Emmy enters the office right when Miss B is calling her a liar and a long lunch taker. Emmy, turning red with anger of hearing being called something she declared she was absolutely NOT, asks what's going on. Miss B, who is never scared, replied "you lied to us and I'm taking this personally". Miss B then provides a note that Emmy wrote and had taped on the door of her meeting room that the ERG meeting (that she was supposed to be at for an hour) was canceled. She then made the accusation that Emmy had used the meeting as an excuse to take an overextended lunchbreak.

Then Bobbi, having no rat in the race, felt the need to chime in that the treatment of Emmy was wrong and then proceeded to tell Miss B she should stay out of it and the issue doesn't concern her. This soon resulted in not only a verbal altercation between Emmy and Miss B, who was hangry and could have gone to lunch on her own, but a violent verbal altercation between Miss

B and Bobbi where physical threats were made before I stepped in the middle and sent the two fighters to their respective office corners. This caused me to have my first staff meeting, which covered conflict resolution, office rules, HR policies, office suspension and resulted in Emmy filing a "complaint of harassment" naming "decimation" of character... yes, decimation not defamation. Emmy would go on to feel bullied and isolated by the others in the office, which furthered her antics.

The bottomline was Emmy would find a way to not work. She went as far as finding seminars to attend that were irrelevant to her job. She would let me know she had signed up and was on her way to the seminar five minutes before it started. Furthermore, it became evident she had no multitasking skills, was disorganized, hadn't been scheduling The Ringmaster's calendar, was not reserving conference rooms for his meetings, and the work she actually completed was done incorrectly. The entire time, her focus had been completing the duties of president of her ERG during the time she was supposed to work as a receptionist.

Needless to say, it was a great joy when I was able to deliver the news to Emmy that we would no longer need her services, or in her case, she was being written off the show. The funny part of this farewell is that she wanted an encore...she came back the next day with a pair of used Easter white slingback pumps, in her hand as a gift to me if I would give her another chance. This is no lie, and just as you're probably saying "whaat?" you are feeling my sentiments exactly. She knew I was a shoe lover and when she brought them to me, she said "I only wore them once and I cleaned them with alcohol, and they are an 8.5". Of course, I declined without hesitation for every reason you can think of, but when she insisted that I try them on...it was just weird. Emmy "take a bow" because the curtain is closed.

Lesson #1

As a new manager, Emmy not only exposed my management flaws but taught me a few lessons in the meantime.

1) Document Everything: Email will be your best friend in this process along with keeping an electronic file where you write all interactions and violations you witnessed with this employee. It's always best if you can, to have someone else in the room when you speak to them, so they don't twist your words and always, always, copy someone on the emails you send to them. Even if you have to BCC because it will serve as a backup, remember there are two sides of the story and then there is the truth. That BCC or CC, will prove to be the truth.

2) Set Clear Expectations: For example, this is what is expected and if this doesn't happen, then this is the result or consequence.

3) Verify hearsay with all parties involved present. If it is said someone said I was to do this, call that person in front of them to confirm it. Then document the entire conversation.

4) Be firm and stick to the facts when discussing anything with them. Also be careful because once they understand you have them figured out, then they will sense their days are numbered and will begin to seek repentance to buy them time. Don't buy it, this is another trick.

The Pretender

The second receptionist was not the model employee, nor did she ever portray to be; however, she seemed like she could bring value to the office with the help of some professional development. She came highly recommended from her former employer who was a known businessman in the community, where she had served as a receptionist for his realtor office. Additionally, she was a former intern and The Ringmaster thought she would be worth the investment. I remembered her from her intern days because she was good friends with my assistant.

At that time, I observed her to be quiet and pleasant but I did have reservations about her resume and the tone of the recommendation letter, which seemed to lean more on the side of pity than endorsement. When I say a pity letter, meaning it was like her former boss was saying *she's a decent girl but I can't have her here anymore because she messes everything up, so anything I can do to get her a job elsewhere without tarnishing my reputation, I'll do it.* This tone from the letter we received would prove to be true but The Ringmaster was all about potential and working with people he felt he could mold. I couldn't complain because I didn't have much experience in the area but I was actually a hard worker, a quick learner, and a good person.

This receptionist, who I will refer to as Pretender, turned out to need extreme development. Though she graduated with her bachelor's degree in accounting and had a job in providing secretarial work, she did not know how to do a lot of basic things but would say she did; hence the nickname, Pretender. The good part of it all was she was willing to learn, so we taught her...even if it meant teaching the same lesson several times. Anyway, she grew on Danille and I, so we accepted her. Everyone has flaws but you can make things work when you and the person in question are aware of their shortcomings, because you can prepare for it. I knew she did not pay attention to detail, so before she submitted anything to The Ringmaster, it was established she needed to have either Danille or me look over it and make corrections before submission. It's simple things like having rapport and humbleness that makes it easy to work with people, regardless of their abilities.

Overall, we had good times with The Pretender. Sure, her perception was off, like the time she told us her mom could "pass". Pass is a term mainly used in the Black community referring to a Black person's skin tone that is similar to a white person's, so the term "could pass" means the person could be mistaken for a white person or could pass for white. However, when we actually met her mother, she had the same complexion/skin tone as Michelle

Obama. That was our first warning that we needed to verify her claims and there would be many stories she would tell and we would indulge because we found them entertaining. The most interesting ones were during lunch time when she would tell us about her sexcapades. It was like watching television for me. I was entertained and always looked forward to getting the "tea" with my meal. After a while the stories gave us more information about her and opened up a whole can of worms that I care not to mention, out of respect for our then relationship.

Trickiness of Manager-Subordinate Friendships

Fast forward, in completing a department reorganization, The Ringmaster moved The Pretender from receptionist to recruitment coordinator and this would be the turn of the relationship. My job went from manager to micromanager as she simply was not qualified because she did not have the capacity to work independently.   She would become so sidetracked with a new love interest that she would literally forget to register and attend recruitment events and would schedule other staff to attend events at places the company was not invited to attend. It was bad and that wasn't even half of it.

The Pretender's non performance reached the point where we had to have daily meetings with her to go over her tasks for the day and then throughout the day to check her progress to ensure she was even working. We had to eventually record the times and reason she left the office as she would leave for a restroom visit and not return until an hour later. When she did complete her work it would be so poorly done, that it had to be redone, and because it would take her twice as long to finish, it became quicker to divide it up and do it ourselves. Her work's multitude of errors became unbearable. All the while, our work relationship began to diminish when she met a new guy and out of concern, Danille and I advised her to leave him. Not sure if it was the way we said it or whether we said it at all but our relationship went from socializing while working to just working in the same office. Our lunch together ceased because the frustration of her not completing her work on time created more work for us and I'm sure she had gotten tired of hearing from us about how she had messed up, yet again.

It is a sticky situation to be in because anytime you have to micromanage, the problem is already out of control. Eventually, I had to write a letter of reprimand for her because she simply did not do her work when she was present and had excessive absences without prior notice. The complaints rolled in from staff members in our department and throughout the company of her disorganization and lack of communication. The breaking point was a recruitment luncheon was planned and less than a week before the event, we discovered she had not completed an agenda nor ordered any food, despite saying she did during daily meetings. This is where you must have documentation and you have to document no matter if you are on good or bad terms with someone. You can never let personal relationships influence your performance as a manager.

The fact was I had a 52-page printout of her Facebook activity during work hours when she claimed she was working but wasn't meeting deadlines nor recruiting nor booking recruitment events. She had gone back to school to get her masters degree and would sit and do her coursework openly at her desk. An electronic calendar to remind her of daily tasks was set up to help her and a detailed explanation, along with examples were given for each task assigned, which she was asked to repeat to ensure comprehension, yet she would blatantly not complete the work. Interns were assigned to assist her but she refused their help, in fear they would outperform her.

Work relationships are important and if there is good rapport, work life is a lot easier; however, when it turns bad, it contributes to toxicity. It is often stated that marriage is hard because you constantly have to work at it as each partner experiences ups and downs inside and outside of the relationship. The same can be said for any relationship where you interact with someone on a daily basis and work relationships are no different. I am not saying work relationships are on the same level as marriages, I am making a comparison that like marriages, work relationships require a sense of cultivation, including compromise and constant communication to be healthy. When these relationships grow sour, it causes turnover, emotional stress, decreased productivity, and role confusion.

In my work relationship with The Pretender, I did not define the lines. As her manager, I should have drawn and enforced the boundaries but I let my interest in her exciting life take precedence over her performance and her personal struggles with work-life balance. I relied on our comradery to guide, even though from the beginning I knew she needed additional development and hands-on management. When she did not like what I said about her personal choice in life, she expressed it through her work performance. My personal thoughts of her provided grace to her shortcomings until it became a burden for me, then I enforced my management authority. I made the mistake of blurring the lines when the relationship was never a true friendship to me but a work friendship, which may have been misconstrued on the opposing end.

The result of this strained work friendship played out at an out-of-town recruiting trip. We sent The Pretender and one of our interns, Opal, to another city on behalf of our department which had staff from other departments of our organization's recruitment team present. Opal was really there as backup representative, in case The Pretender did not show up.

While the event was taking place, I got word from a member of the company's recruitment team that The Pretender was there; however, she arrived late, and gave a "piss-poor" presentation. This individual had worked with her at local recruitment events and previously complained about her behavior but this time they called saying "Why did y'all send her?...she is making your department look bad." They proceeded to tell me she was also making derogatory remarks about me, saying I was "abusing her" and "yelling" at her. Evidently, she then became irate when they told her they didn't believe the bad things she was saying about me and she then threatened to harm me. This later led to a conversation between a company executive and The Ringmaster about her representation of the department and how her behavior and performance was negatively affecting the organization's intern and employee recruitment efforts.

The Pretender was acting out because the work friendship had failed and she no longer had the support from me, which she desperately needed with balancing the aspects of her life. Again this is testament to how we have to separate the behavior from the person because she was a good person and pleasant to work with until things came to this devastating end. Also, there should have been some communication between us once the relationship began to change to salvage it or renegotiate the terms of where we were at the present time. Being the manager, the responsibility was mine to address the blurred lines and restate the new terms of performance expectations, which I failed to do.

No matter what job I have, I take it seriously, so I was infuriated to hear she had been defaming me. Then the fact she threatened to cause physical harm to me, sent me over the edge to the point of no return. When she arrived back in town to the office, I did not make it harder for her, I just ran out of grace and mercy. I dealt with her on an as needed basis and ramped up my documentation. I would only speak to her when someone else was in the room to ensure I had a witness, since I was being accused of saying and doing things I had not done towards her and since she had made a threat to harm me. Did I think she would get physical with me, I don't know but I did not put it past her nor was I scared if she decided to enact. I am certain you have experienced a loss of a work friendship because of a change in work performance or some other work related issue. This is a common interaction in any type of workplace and if not fixed, leads to the full toxicity that will poison the work environment.

The spread of The Pretender's negativity was felt by our interns as well, particularly Opal. While the two were on the recruitment trip, Danille made a major discovery. As we were processing some paperwork for Opal, Danille found her emergency contact. Her face froze and she said "You are not going to believe this...oh my God!" I said "what?!" She proceeded to tell me the person on Opal's emergency contact was not a family member but her boyfriend whose name she recognized from many stories we were told. Opal's boyfriend was The Pretender's daughter's father! The irony and the coincidence.

To make a long story short, the two didn't fight on the trip. I don't remember if they even figured out the one major thing they had in common that day, but they did eventually find out. If I remember correctly, Danille told

Opal. And let's just say, when they say there are two sides to every story...well we heard a whole other side about The Pretender's kid daddy drama compared to the one she originally told us during our lunchtime stories. Danille and I soon found our entertainment replacement during lunch time with Opal's stories of the triangle of Opal, The Pretender, and the boyfriend.

Sooner than later the altercations between The Pretender and the boyfriend made its way into the office with The Pretender mistreating Opal. We were extremely impressed with how Opal handled herself with The Pretender in the office, yet not surprised at how she reacted to Opal. I think embarrassment really hit when Opal became pregnant by the boyfriend and had a better experience with him as the father than The Pretender. It was crazy times because The Pretender had painted this guy as a disgusting criminal and it all had been a lie per the proof Opal had shown us.

Regardless, Danille and I alerted The Ringmaster so he would be aware of the situation, in the event it escalated beyond the insults hurled at Opal by The Pretender. Danille and I worked together in trying to keep the interactions of the two separate. Additionally, Danille had a conversation with Opal to set some ground rules and reiterate a professional environment as not to bring their personal drama to the workplace. On the other end, The Ringmaster and I had a conversation with The Pretender to ensure the same. Danille was there to point out some of the mistreatment of Opal by The Pretender, due to their personal relationship, as to further explain the prohibited behavior in the office. Overall, the two adhered to peace in the office though their tension was present as their personal issues grew.

Lesson #2

What I learned from this situation is communication is key and it takes many forms. Documentation definitely played an integral part in communicating expected behaviors and reporting unwanted behavior. I learned as a manager, you have to be transparent with your subordinates to earn and maintain full trust. When work relationships begin to turn sour, enhance the communication to identify areas of improvement and seek resolve. Additionally, as a manager, you hold the sole responsibility in setting the pace for work friendships and you have to be able to communicate the perimeters of that relationship to ensure lines are not blurred and the work environment remains professional.

I also learned communication can lead to negative paths, such as gossip and isolation. What you say to people and about people travels and could ruin relationships, cause harm, and ultimately lead to job probation and termination. We have to be smart in how and to whom we express our frustrations and the stories we choose to share as they could have negative effects, regardless of the intent. If you have a personal issue with someone, it is best to discuss it directly with the goal to find an amicable resolution to enjoy a cordial work atmosphere.

Lastly, listen to people when their actions change; people often have a better grasp of what they can handle. The mistake was promoting The Pretender into a position she clearly could not handle and a discussion should have taken place prior and a plan of action determined. Basically, knowing she needed development as a receptionist, we set her up for failure in giving her the recruitment position without providing her with the tools to successfully perform in that role. You cannot turn a turtle into a giraffe. Nothing is wrong with a turtle but you must respect that it is exactly what it was created to be. You can bring it to higher levels but cannot expect it to eat from the trees because it wasn't created to do that. Some people get overwhelmed with additional responsibilities and have no understanding of how to handle them on their own, no matter how you try to develop them or give them support. If you try to pressure them, they will only find some way to get out of it and they will eventually shut down. When you see this happening, do not push them, let them be great where they are comfortable.

Insubordination

I thought I had met and had my last dance with the devil when Big Sister had graduated and left our collegiate sorority chapter. Her departure was like music to my ears, I think the song playing, in my mind, was "Hit the Road Jack" and I was singing loud and proud (to myself) "and don'thca' come back no mooooorrrrre!" Oh, the air seemed more crisp and the sky more blue, I had pep in my step and roll in my neck. Though I dreaded the situation at the time, I must admit it made me better, gave me experience, and matured me. Collegiate days in a sorority were slight torment, just the sight of Big Sister tormented me. With her departure I thought the best was yet to come for the rest of my life…nothing but happy days as an adult, in a new city, with a master's degree, and a promising job. Oh but if I knew then what I know now, Big Sister was just the beginning…and I thank her for preparing me for my future. A few short years later, the bumps and bruises I endured from Big Sister would be the source for my survival of the antics I would incur from Medusa, Bobbi Blockhead, Squatter, and The Pretender.

One late afternoon, with my ears glued to the door, I heard the best news. Bobbi Blockhead had received another job! I think I actually received the Holy Ghost that day in my office; it was like my prayers had suddenly been answered. I immediately thought about Psalms 98:4 and began seeing a scene from Snow White when the birds were singing, animals grazing, and people smiling and dancing with their hands joined in a circle. I actually broke out in a dance myself, it was like twirling in a circle with my left leg slightly cocked at a 90 degree angle.

Yes! I immediately ran to my desk and called my mom on the phone to tell her the good news. It was like fire shut up in my bones. Now all I needed was for Medusa to get a job and I would be in the clear and this news of

Bobbi would be just the motivation she would need to move on and out. I knew Medusa was upset she didn't get a job first, but *it's not where you're at, it's where you are going!* At least that's the outlook I had for her and it was like comfort food to me. I begin to think about what selection from my virtual jukebox would I play for her when she leaves…"Ding Dong the witch is dead"? I just decided to embrace this celebratory moment and let the future take care of itself.

Bobbi tried to keep her departure a secret. She kept up the clique's obvious antics of changing the subject whenever I came around, everyone immediately silent and stiff when I came into the front office, all the symptoms of "secret keeping". It didn't bother me because I already knew and I was so happy for her and even more happy for myself. The Bible says 'the enemy will come at you one way but will flee seven ways.' This was way number one in their fleet, hallelujah!

I would be lying if I said her leaving was swift and peaceful, but I kept the end result in mind. There was one last conspiracy they had for me; I guess it was one for the road. The gist of it was The Ringmaster wanted to make room for the executive director to move into our office suite. This meant we, the staff, would need to switch offices. Bobbi was to move to the storage room turned front office in the suite. Medusa was to move to Bobbi's office, and the executive director would then move into Medusa's office. This meant the ball was in Bobbi's court to get the process going.

Trick #3: Conspire

She did everything she could to not move by using every excuse in the book. Medusa didn't want to move because she was moving into a much smaller office in the back of the suite and the narcissist in her perceived it as a demotion. She encouraged Bobbi not to move since she was quitting and convinced her to use the excuse of not having enough time. The most disappointing thing was the two decided that if the pressure came to move, then Blockhead Bobbi should tell The Ringmaster that I needed to move her because I was her supervisor. This was Trick #3. The devil has never been smart, just timely. Thanks to my superb eavesdropping skills, I heard them hatch this whole plan. Secondly, their intentions were blatantly obvious. The Ringmaster told me to encourage Bobbi to move and if she refused, then to write her up for insubordination.

I just happened to have a better plan. I'd do exactly what they wanted me to do, I'd move her myself. I went into double time, doing my work and then the last hours of the day, I would move her stuff from one office to the other. I told her, 'hey The Ringmaster told me to help you move. I know you are busy, so whatever would take the most time for you to move, you can just tell me and I will do that for you'. Unbeknownst to them, they had taught me how to play their games. My thoughts were *Girl, you have a part-time job, you ain't busy! You talk more hours than you work, but that's cool.* My plan worked, she couldn't pass up giving me the hard jobs such as cleaning out the storage room that she was to move into, which would become the front office again. I dedicated a Friday for clean-up day and got that front office ready for her to move in. When she arrived at the office the following Monday, she didn't know what to do. Her plan was unfolding in front of her eyes.

Trick #4: Play Busy

When their first trick did not work, Medusa told her to stick with *she's too busy to move*. I was way ahead of them, I helped her move completely. Bobbi's entire argument was that she didn't have the time to clean out the front office in order to move her things from her office. The Ringmaster had told her several months prior to clean out that front office and she never did because she didn't want to. Now, she went on a campaign that it was too much and he was putting too much on her to move and do her work in a timely manner. Her statement was the same regardless of an office move as she had never done her work in a timely manner before because she was preoccupied with keeping tabs on her boyfriend and talking to Medusa.

Where there is a will there's a way, and I have a strong will. Once I snatched the excuse of the front office not being available for her to move and then moving her things into the office, it dismantled their plan. When Medusa realized I had cleaned the front office and had volunteered to help Bobbi move her stuff into the front office, she went to The Ringmaster and argued that I shouldn't be moving Bobbi into the front office because I had more important work to do.

Trick #5: Throw Someone Underneath the Bus

Medusa told The Ringmaster, Bobbi hadn't planned to move in the first place and she was holding up the moving process. Here is evidence of why she is affectionately referred to as Medusa. Remember, I told you The Ringmaster tells me everything. Medusa then comes to me with miraculous deadlines for the projects her and I were working on together. Needless to say, *Project Move* was put on halt, but not for long. Bobbi finally started moving because she could no longer keep up the facade and The Ringmaster wanted the executive director moved at a certain date.

Off to a very slow start, moving one thing at a time, so I told Bobbi, 'let me help you because a deadline has been set and we need to abide by that, so that I don't get in trouble, because ultimately, I'm your supervisor'. So I began to move all of her files and what I did was take them out of the file cabinet and place them at the entrance of her new office, so she now had to get them out of the way in order to enter and exit. With the items there, not to mention they were confidential files, she had to move with haste. She worked hard sorting through those files plus the ones I moved into the adjoining storage room. Now the only thing she had to move was the personal items from her desk and I gave her a box and a time to have that out because I was now giving her office key to Medusa to move her things in Bobbi's newly former office.

Lesson #3

The fact is insubordination is a blatant disrespect of authority which causes major transgressions in the workplace. The lesson from this story was sometimes you have to beat them at their own game, with their own rules. Written reprimands are not always the only solution. In this case, I could have written her up as well because she was insubordinate and I had to move her myself. In fact, that may have been the best solution, kill a bird with two stones. Nonetheless, she was leaving anyway, so the disciplinary action would not have made much of a difference in this case. More importantly, I was just enthralled with the idea she was leaving that nothing else mattered. One down, one to go was how I looked at it.

Ever heard someone say "you just can't make this stuff up", well that is how I felt at times dealing with certain people on the job. I have watched a lot of television in my day because I like to be entertained and escape the woes of life. I like to watch dramas because I am drama free and like to keep everything around me that way. Basically, I watch television to experience things that don't happen in my life; I like television for the exaggeration of personalities and circumstances. I get to experience it from a far and not be involved in it and it ultimately has zero effect on me. Well some of the craziest things I have experienced have come from the workplace and it has, when speaking with friends, made me say "You won't believe what I'm about to tell you, it's crazy cause I can't make this up." Why can't we make it up, because it is so far fetched from how we would normally act or expect others to act. That is only true if you are not one of the exaggerated characters that TV life is based off of.

The Lesson

Work relationships are as dramatic as those watched on television. We make up to break up, use and abuse, agree and disagree, ban together and isolate, and forgive and forget with the best of them. It is the nature of relationships to have its ups and downs but the key to keeping the pleasantry takes work on both ends and communication is the underlying feature. The beauty of work friendships are they are beneficial for organizational and individual performance and yet do not require the devotion of personal friendships.

Whether the workplace friendship is among peers or job levels, the positive connection is beneficial. Manager-to-subordinate friendships increase socialization and add fun to the workplace and have an overall positive impact on work attitude. No matter the parties of the workplace friendship, it is priceless to employees and the organization. However, when these relationships are non-existent, estranged, or used in negative ways, they become the perpetuation of toxicity.

Workplace cliques are definitely evidence of the bird brood; they are a group of folks bonded together with the potential to socially isolate others and/or create barriers of entry through ostracism. These cliques, formed through similar social identities or common goals, can be permanent friendships or temporary comrades focused on accomplishing a task. Either way, the existence of them automatically causes separatism and has the power to limit communication to outsiders, which ultimately ignores the person and diminishes them to their specific work role. Are workplace cliques all bad? No, but even the unintentional effects contribute to the toxicity in the work environment.

My experience with the girls on the job was a mixture of it all. I found it amusing how quickly Medusa's clique of Miss B, Bobbi, and Emmy wanted to be friendly with me after being dissed by each other and being the casualty under Medusa's bus. I had also become accustomed to the gossip about me that would suddenly turn into pure silence which would overcome their robust conversation when I walked in the room. Despite the negative thoughts and words they said about me, it never stopped me from doing my job and I never allowed it to hold a professional grudge towards them. However, I did let it limit the lack of communication and I succumbed to some immature actions as a result. The silver lining is that I learned from it and used it as professional development for future jobs, just like you should if you ever encounter any of these situations.

At most, it behooved me to stay out of politics to keep my sanity and always remain on the right side of the truth. Their arguments with each other and Medusa were frequent and reminded me of the time I witnessed a woman physically beaten by a man outside my apartment, just to see her in affectionate embrace with her attacker the next day. Had I taken a side, I would have been hated by both parties, so I tried my best to stay clear of the drama but I enjoyed hearing the stories.

Remaining neutral is your best option in surviving in these environments, choosing not to align yourself too closely to any politics and cliques. You always want to be fluid. There is a serious price you pay to be in the cliche. They can turn on you and also if you don't back them up or do what they want you to do, right or wrong, they can gang up and destroy your character. They could also expose something you may have said in secret or something you said out of stupidity as to agree with them. Either way, you must know that energy is transferable, so if you hang with negative people you will become negative. If you hang with people who constantly talk about people, one day they'll talk about you. I'm not saying spend your work time alone, you definitely need at least one good work best friend, and we'll talk about that in a later chapter, but you need to be careful who you associate yourself with at work and walk the fine line between cliches and friendships.

Benjamin Schneider (1982) argued toxic environments can change but it has to start with the changing of the people before the structures and processes change. He says we must seek explanation in people, not in the results of their behavior. Academician R. Morrison (2009) stated workplace friendships are more likely to develop among women because they thrive on social and emotional support, whereas men are focused more on career and functional aspects of how they can accomplish a job. Therefore, this may explain why most of my toxicity came from the mouths and actions of women. Not to excuse the men because some of them contributed to the toxicity but it was in a different manner.

Scholar F.T. McAndrew (2013) stated the goal of gossip is to ostracize and isolate others in a competitive way as to damage their reputation and ability to become a part of a particular group. Gossip tends to be an aggression tactic for women. We know this to be of huge importance because as stated before, our sense of belonging is a basic human need and for someone to seek to remove that need from another person can have psychological effects on them, not just on the job but outside. Especially when you consider that everyone working comes with prior experience, which could include hurts and pains. If they have experienced that before, imagine the damage it does to them to experience it again. They say 'loose lips sink ships' but loose cliques sink ships when it comes to the workplace.

Workplace cliques can form naturally just as regular cliques. It is important to recognize the power that friendships and cliques have in the work environment and I hope you will seek ways to use these social relationships for positive change, especially in the midst of toxicity.

The final lesson learned from the experiences in this chapter was the effects of lying. I was lied to and lied on, as I know many of you could probably testify. A lot of times, the lying occurs without your personal witnessing but its after effects is the evidence. The Squatter, Bobbi, Medusa, Miss B, and The Pretender all told lies about me and each other and to everyone in the office for personal gain. Though some people like to categorize the tales of untruths, it is all the same and leads
to suspicion, distrust, animosity, isolation, and low morale, all characteristics of a toxic work environment.

It is important to understand that lying is just not a negative action, but is a common social-functional behavior advanced in workplace relationships. It is a threat management behavioral response to attacks a person feels is on their identity as it relates to the work environment. What this means is anytime someone feels threatened, whether by your mere existence or any experience or lack of, they will seek to save themselves through lying. Again, do not take it personal but ensure you stay aware, document, and form positive alliances.

IT'S ME, NOT YOU

5   DREAMS, SHAMS, & SCAMMERS

I never knew I would be a writer as a child, especially because I despised it and reading even more. I would half do my writing assignments, conjuring plans to fool my teachers into thinking I really read the books when I submitted my book report. I was a model student but somehow I figured out ways to cut corners in areas that I didn't like and it would work. Teachers would sing my praises and my classmates would call me "teacher's pet" or "goodie two-shoes" because the teachers knew, from the quality of their report, they (the other students) had not read the book and I was now showing them up because it appeared I had. If they would have known I barely read two chapters because I was too busy watching television, it would have been the end to my squeaky clean image and lowered their expectations of me. Somehow back then, people associated being smart with having the ability and pleasure to read and write well. It is true but it is not absolute because in third grade I tested into sixth grade reading and comprehension, so the ability was there but the joy was not. However, school was a system I knew my way around quite well.

Though I was told I had to be serious about schooling, and I was, deep inside I was a dreamer. I saw other kids chastised for daydreaming and not being focused, so I did what I could to conceal the fact I was guilty of the same pleasure they found in their imaginations. In those days, you were either focused on school or not and there was no in between. However, I considered myself to be the exception. I did my homework to the tune of television. There was no "do your homework and then watch tv" like others were told in their households. I did my homework alongside watching The Cosby Show, game shows, and whatever else that came on television which grabbed my attention.

As a child I had my own double-consciousness, a couch-potato and a scholar. I read slowly (I still do) and at times it took me several reads to comprehend, which is why I probably developed a hatred towards reading and writing. Writing made me think in real time but television allowed me to imagine and understand things beyond my scope. I remember in elementary, we had these big, horizontal, rectangular windows that lined the classroom, facing the playground and street. To open them, you would pull the handle towards you, like you were opening an oven. It was a gift in the spring time and a curse in winter if your desk was in the row next to them. At the beginning of the school year (August/September) and at the end of the year (April/May), I always wanted to sit by the big classroom windows so I could look out and daydream. When we would have in-class writing assignments, I developed a hidden rebellion because it took me away from the freedom I had grown to love in dreaming.

Being the only Black child in my classroom and one of few in the entire school in a town population of roughly 55,000 with a 1% Black and 95% White population, I learned quickly my culture at home wasn't always understood in scholastics. It wasn't like today where tolerance and diversity was celebrated or even acknowledged. For many of my classmates, I was their only interaction or access to the Black culture and no one cared because I was the minority. If they were curious, it was never shown, so for me not to stick out more than the obvious, I assimilated into their culture, their way of being, their way of doing things. It was suppression and I played a part in it.

I remember hating February because it was Black History Month and my teachers felt obligated to have one activity/assignment related to it only in the classes they had me as a student. It was extremely uncomfortable because the other students would voice their complaints because they knew their other classes didn't have this half-hearted lesson. I remember a classmate saying "Why do we have to learn about that (referring to Martin Luther King, Jr.), we are not Black?". It was doubly uncomfortable because my family, my mom especially, had taught me about Black history beyond the poster child of Dr. King, so I didn't need the annual artificial appreciation of Black culture from my teachers who knew nothing other than the "I Have a Dream" speech. It was uncomfortable for me and unfair to Black and American culture alike, to the point I recall speaking to my teacher after class to let them know we didn't have to talk about Black history because it wasn't fair to the class to learn about it simply because I was Black.

I was fine with my double-consciousness of being Black in a White world and my secular dreams in the academic world, that I didn't need resentment added on. My sentiments were to be at peace playing their game because it is clear there wasn't a genuine sense to understand or embrace my culture.

I know my teachers had a good-heart and by no means meant any ill-will or disrespect. Looking back, they just wanted to make me feel included but in my mind, I already was; however, singling me out was excluding me in more ways than one. When I was sequestered to in-class writing assignments about our experiences to a certain subject, sometimes I acted out through my writing by telling my truth and as a result suffered from a lower grade because my perspective seemed far fetched from the monotonic interpretations of my classmates' writings.

I remember in the third or fourth grade being given an essay assignment to write on how we wanted a loved one to stop smoking. I asked the teacher if I could write about something else because I was told by my family 'we don't tell the family business to strangers and the people at school'. In an effort to not out my grandmother and not get in trouble because I wanted my grandma NOT to do something by telling her how wrong it was (which is a no-no in the Black household), I originally said I didn't know anyone who smoked. It didn't work.

I sat there wrestling with myself on how I was going to write an essay that spoke badly about my grandma's smoking habit that she could potentially see, while trying to not get in trouble at school at the same time for not doing what the teacher said. I came up with the brilliant idea to make up a story and if my teacher sent this letter to my grandma, like she said she would, as long as it had a good grade on it, my family would care less that it was made up. However, I struggled to make up something that was good enough as my teacher watched me like a hawk. I just came to the conclusion, 'she wants the truth, I'm going to give her the truth', so I wrote the essay out of defiance and a realness I knew could get me into trouble because it was not what had been asked of us. I felt a little guilty after turning it in because I knew my teacher had high expectations of me and I felt my sweet image may have been tarnished by the things I wrote in the essay, but it was the truth and I knew she couldn't understand and because of that, she may look at me differently.

A few weeks later my teacher announced the essays had been submitted to a city-wide essay competition and two entries from our class had been selected: one that was a genuine plea for a father to stop smoking and how the son was willing to help him stop and one that was not a plea but well-written, expressive and of a different perspective than the intent of the essay contest. I sat in my seat a little regretful because I had let my feelings get in the way of my studious image, a good grade, and a chance to win (I liked to win, period). Then the teacher announces Chris Ruby's name and hands him a certificate for his essay about wanting to help his dad to stop smoking and then turns to me. She tells the class about how impressed the judges were of my essay and my experience with my grandmother and how she knew it would win because it was the best essay in the class. I was shocked and this would set the stage for other shocks of this magnitude that would be birthed out of my suppression of my cultural differences during my public school writing career.

When I reached seventh grade, I learned about different forms of literature through Ms. Mitchell, a teacher, whom I loved and trusted until she kept the only copy of my beloved original poem and moved away to Portland, never to return again. In that class, she introduced me to poetry. She encouraged us to dream and imagine beyond what we could see and then compare it to our reality. I was in awe of this class where I didn't have to disguise my imagination because it was appreciated. It was at that time I fell in love with poetry and John Boyle O'Reilly's *The Cry of a Dreamer*. His words let me know as a poor, shy, little Black girl, it was okay to dream, because "There is nothing sweet in the city but the patient lives of the poor...For a dreamer lives forever, and a toiler dies in a day".

I took that refrain to heart and with the support of my family, I kept dreaming. I had dreams that developed into short-term and long-term goals and I voiced them as my plans. I remember in the 10th grade sitting in class telling my friends my plan to be rich. How I was going to attend Kansas State University because at that time a lot of their athletes were being considered for professional sports teams. Since the school was a predominantly white institution, I would stick out and would develop a relationship and would marry a football or basketball player who would later make it into the league. If KState didn't work out, my backup plan was Michigan because of the Fab 5. I would get a basketball player who would make it to the NBA, either way, that was my plan to wealth. I would take care of the house and manage it while he played professional sports. The business degree I would earn while in college would help me to manage our joint business ventures along with the household. I had it all figured out and my friends were on board. They were happy for me and gave assurance it would happen and for me not to forget about them when I "make it".

In those days I believed and was thoroughly convinced. When senior year came around my ambition was deflated when I realized KState hadn't offered enough scholarship money to pay my freshman year, Michigan's tuition was unaffordable, and there were not enough resources to help me attend either school for free. On top of this disappointment, my mom wasn't financially able to pay for my education, she didn't make enough and I didn't have a rich uncle in Bel-Air, so how was college going to even work for me? I had good grades and extracurricular activities but big scholarships were not awarded to me.

My mom made too much for a Pell Grant but not enough to pay for a semester. My teacher, counselors and family had high hopes for me but hope was not in the form of scholarship checks. I felt I couldn't let them down, they were always bragging about me. I had cousins who looked up to me, what example would I be to settle into an ordinary life like everyone else we had seen? That would mean my peak was now and deep down inside I knew my dreams were too big for my future not to be bright.

Then in the knick of time, like He always does, God showed up. I got a letter in the mail for a full-ride to college. It may not have been a division one school, like I had dreamed, but it was college and I would have to make the best of this opportunity. What I understood was that my dream to wealth via my pro-athlete husband had to be deferred. My reality was I'd settle for an ordinary guy with a southern edge who'd eventually end our collegiate relationship because of the insecurity of not being worthy of my potential. I didn't see it but his family did and they constantly warned him about messing up my future to the point he decided it wouldn't work between us because he was worried that one day I'd realize it and leave him.

At the time, it was a hard pill to swallow but in hindsight it was God's way of freeing me to walk on the path of His ultimate plan for my life. I was permitted to dream again and released to believe the sky was the limit, just like my family had told me when I was a child. I picked up and moved to another city where I thought all of my dreams would come true. In the first year, it seemed like it would. I was doing things I could not have done back home because the city was so big and full of promise and opportunity.

Shams & Scams

In this new city, I found people who looked like me, who shared the same culture, but were from families who were wealthy. These people were in charge and folks my age were engaging and succeeding in entrepreneurship.. They had a hustle and there was so much life, so many possibilities and opportunities and I now could see how some of my dreams could come true. I remember getting a job with a sports agency in the summer. I was around professional athletes and my high school dream to *richly road* was back in view.

Then during graduate school, I received an internship at a small public relations firm catering to athletes and local celebrities. As Celine Deion sang, "it's all coming back to me now". The PR firm was owned by Conny, a late 30's Black woman who was cool, business savvy, and ghetto all at the same time. She was from New York but had spent some time in the early 90's as a dancer for MC Hammer, who I was a major fan of growing up. She was married to a stout country boy, who stood about 5 '9, an inch shorter than Conny, who also served as her business partner and muscle for the firm.

Conny was inspirational. I was an intern along with three other college girls including Jorie, from Los Angeles who became a friend. We often talked about how inspiring Conny was to us as young Black women in business school. She was an entrepreneur who demanded respect from everyone, despite their celebrity and economic status. She made things happen and we were in awe learning from her. Jorie and I had planned to learn all we could from Conny and make contacts through her network because we were going to become partners and start a business of our own with more organization and class. We figured we could leverage our youthfulness and looks to get clientele and our education and experience to maintain clients.

I loved that job. I was able to do marketing, event planning, and even modeling. I was on photo shoots, partying with celebrities...I was living the life I had dreamt. Jorie and I had become Conny's favorites, so we were getting to help out on more events and with more clients. I had even met a model who would give me the lowdown on the entertainment industry. She had been in multiple music videos and had partied with top celebrities. She even had children from Hall of Famers, a huge house in an upscale neighborhood, and shared with us she had never worked a 9-5 job and was doing modeling just to make a name for herself. I was in awe. I had even thought about taking a page from her life's book but thought about the example that would be for my cousins and how disappointing my family and friends would be that I settled and didn't live out my dreams.

There was more work for me and for a moment I thought the PR firm was my key to success. Then reality started to settle in when one of the interns said she was quitting because Conny had not paid her. She warned Jorie and I that our beloved Conny, who had taken us under her wing and was showing us the ropes, the Conny who gave me Versace for my birthday, the Conny who invited us to Thanksgiving at her house because we had no family in town and couldn't afford to go home, the Conny who was giving us extra money to model for her clients, the Conny who had given us clout at certain bars that picked up my tab for my birthday party, was not who she said she was...unbelievable.

We understood our co-worker's disdain for not getting paid, but we had received our paychecks and so much opportunity that we had no desire to quit and unite with her when we had not experienced the Conny she had spoken of. As the co-worker's efforts to expose Conny fizzled, things slowly started to unravel. Clients from the firm started calling for Conny on the general line and she insisted we tell them she wasn't there, when she was sitting in the next room. Next, Conny decided to relocate the office due to mold, which we never saw. It even reached the point where she told us not to answer the door if the landlord tried to talk to us and to be on the lookout, just in case the landlady tried to bombard us when we were getting out of the car to come into the office.

Then on the fateful day, we showed up to the office and it had an eviction notice on the door and it was locked. This was disappointing because without an office, that means we had no job. After numerous calls, Conny responded and told us she had to go out of town but would pay us. Then this dream came crashing down when my paycheck didn't cash. When I asked her, she said there was a mix up with the bank, indicating the bank was at fault and she wrote me another check with an increased amount to cover the NSF fee I was charged by my bank for her check not clearing.

This time I went the next day to her bank, which was 40 minutes away, to cash the check to avoid fees. They told me the check was bad and the account had been closed for some time because it was thousands of dollars in the hole yet checks kept coming in and they were actually looking for her. I was heated, I remember asking the teller if I could file a complaint against Conny for fraud if that would get her arrested and get my money for my paycheck. Needless to say, I had been conned. In fact, we all had been as we would find out months later when the FBI was looking for her because her cons had exceeded three states, which included stolen social security numbers and money, bounced checks, and various forms of other fraudulent activity. It was disheartening because this was the second time I had been burned in pursuing my dreams.

A Sham

Toxicity can also exist in the traditional work environment with the cliques of people and their destructive behavior. My experience with Conny's unethical behavior was a clear exhibition of leadership that creates an undercover toxic environment. It's like boiling frogs; you put them in a pot of cold water and slowly turn up the heat and by the time they realize it, they can't jump out because they're cooked. These types of environments are built on lies from ambitious people who are only in business for themselves. Oftentimes their motives aren't clear but disguised as nurturing tactics as they learn to prey on vulnerable, naive, and desperate people. They are disingenuous with their approaches and lack trust in their shady practices. They take risks and when they feel they are being challenged, quickly the wolf in them peaks or fully surfaces.

Conny wasn't my only experience in dealing with scams. I had actually had a previous encounter with a total sham under the guise of a home-based modeling agency. It was a little less sophisticated than Conny's ring, because at least she had an office and actual clients. This first experience approached me, when I was fresh in a new city with hopes of becoming a model.

I was riding on the fumes of years of comments of how my height, build, and beauty mirrored that of a supermodel. Moving to the big city, I thought this was my chance to be bold and go after my dreams that seemed ions away from the shelter of Nebraska. I'm unsure how it came about but I met this early 30's lady, who we'll call Shaydee, who started a modeling agency called *Perfect 10*. She invited me to events, called me to talk about the modeling industry, took professional pictures of me, and bought me makeup, at her expense because I "was her investment". It wasn't just me, it was other young ladies, who once meeting, didn't fit the traditional model mold, in my opinion. They were on the shorter side of 5 feet, voluptuous, with an edge.

I really thought Shaydee was nice and told my mom about how nice she treated me and how I wanted to be a part of her dream. My mom immediately warned me and told me to be careful as this agency didn't sound legitimate operating from her home, coupled with the fact she had yet to book a job for me. Despite what my mother said, I actually believed in Shaydee and her entrepreneurial effort. I wanted to be a model so badly I was blind to the obvious and didn't want to share anymore information with my mom because her discernment was killing my dream.

One day, Shaydee told me to bring some "sexy" outfits to take pictures but I didn't have any lingerie or other items she had requested. I brought the closest thing I had, which was my sexiest night club outfit, which was a pink mini-skirt and a black sheer blouse that needed a safety pin to keep it closed. I would normally wear the shirt with a black cami underneath to not be exposed.

Shaydee, myself, and the other girls went to a high-end shopping center where there was a beautiful waterfall, which would be the backdrop for my photo shoot. It was there we shot my first modeling portfolio; I was excited. Changing in the car, she told me not to put the cami underneath my sheer blouse. I refused but she began to tell me nothing would show as she wanted to capture the plunging neckline only of the shirt and nothing else. She then said not to wear a bra because it would interrupt the neckline of the blouse and she would Photoshop out anything that appeared. I hesitated but I trusted her and the other girls assured me Shaydee wouldn't put me in any compromising situation. I did what she told me and I was modeling and getting more comfortable with each snap of the camera.

People were walking by giving me compliments and it was happening, I was modeling. Then I noticed a police officer, who was directing traffic, kept staring at me with this lingering look that made me feel uncomfortable. As I continued to change poses, I thought he should be more focused on directing traffic than looking at me. Then I heard Shaydee say "keep your eyes on me, don't look around or down" as she was taking my pictures and verbally guiding my poses. Looking up, an older woman walked by shaking her head in disgust, leaving me baffled because it was contrary to all the other looks and compliments like "you're beautiful....go girl" I had received from the other passersby. Naturally, I glanced down to see what was wrong with me and saw my breasts were exposed. It all made sense, the old lady, the police officer. I stopped posing and immediately fixed my shirt to cover up. Shaydee, disappointed, assured me not to worry about it because she'd Photoshop it out. I was baffled because she knew my breasts were exposed, yet she kept snapping without telling me. Embarrassed, I immediately ended the shoot.

On the car ride back to her house, Shaydee began to tell me how she wanted me to wear clothes like the other girls for my next shoot. They were wearing lingerie. I expressed how uncomfortable wearing such items would be for me as the other girls' butts and boobs were exposed. Persistent, she tried to convince me I could make more money wearing bedroom lingerie because I was "classy looking" compared to the other girls. In defense mode, I began to argue how I wanted to model clothes not lingerie and the fact I had made no money at all because she failed to book a job for me. Sticking with her story, she countered with statements that professional modeling requires exposing my shape and referencing Tyra Banks modeling underwear and lingerie in Victoria's Secret catalogs and how that is widely accepted.

After that conversation, I started understanding more about my mom's reservations and the fact Shaydee had never booked a job for me and wouldn't let me see my pictures from the shoot. She also started reneging on things she had told me. For example, she said I would receive the files from my portfolio but when I asked for them, she denied making that promise.

This situation is an example of what I'm sure others have been through when trying to pursue their career dreams. You want the dream to be a reality so bad you'll do anything to get it. It's the price you pay and meeting others who have achieved it and who promise to help you get there, you begin to think you can use the package they are selling as a stepping stone. *It's the only way and it may just be the break you need.* Wrong! Some people may think you don't have morals but it's not that, it's you have dreams and drive and you are willing to do what it takes to make those dreams a reality. However, I advise you to hold on to a solid support system because it is necessary in making wise decisions. If you can dream it, with hard work, faith, and determination, you will get it with integrity intact.

Realizing Perfect 10 was not rendering any benefits for me, I threatened to quit. That's when Shaydee finally showed me some pictures from my photoshoot and one had my breasts exposed. I reminded her of the promise she made to delete those pictures; she nonchalantly responded she "hadn't gotten to it yet" and immediately turned aggressive. After that, I became real uneasy being around her and the other girls as the agency started to seem less like modeling and more like a front for a service business.

The day we parted ways was when Shaydee wanted all the girls to go to a downtown nightclub and wear provided midriff tops with no bras. She wanted us all to meet at her house to carpool downtown to the venue. I told her I would meet them at the venue which was 15 minutes from my apartment instead of driving 40 minutes to her home first just to drive downtown. She grew upset with me because the other girls didn't have cars and she wanted them to ride with me. At that point, it was finally clear she was trying to operate another business under the disguise of a modeling agency. Additionally, I was finally seeing her real intentions and was fed up with the lying, phone hang ups, and passive aggressive and controlling behavior. I never showed up to her house or the nightclub. As a result, she left me nasty messages and called me several times at which I never answered or returned.

Skipping forward a year, to when Conny gave me the infamous fraud check at a clothing store while picking out clothes for a fashion show. One of Conny's photographers pulled me aside and showed me Perfect 10's website, which included pictures of me. He warned me to be careful of Shaydee, as she was deceitful with plans to operate an online escorting business. The irony was that I had escaped Shaydee's sham and was in the process of quickly discovering I was about to be scammed by Conny.

The Lesson

Knowing about Conny's fraudulent situation, the employment agency had to take action as Knowing about Conny's fraudulent situation, the employment agency had to take action as the internship with the PR firm was through their partnership. Hearing of the news, The Ringmaster offered me an internship in his office. I had no choice but to accept the offer because I needed the money. Again, God to the rescue at the knick of time.

This meant my dream would be deferred again as I transitioned back to an ordinary job to stay afloat. At this time, I began to think my dreams were even too big for me. I would later give modeling another try through a legitimate modeling agency and modeling gigs from a freelance photographer. Neither amounted to anything substantial. I spent over $1,000 to be under the tutelage of a modeling agency just for them to teach me how to apply makeup and lamely walk on a runway. I honestly learned more about posing and walking a runway from religiously watching America's Top Model than this agency. All the jobs they had for me were unpaid, though they received payment for my performance, their service in communicating details about available jobs and events to attend was inaccurate and last minute, accompanied by terrible attitudes, and the price was just too high. In order to book a job, you had to have a card which had your pictures and measurements on it. They refused to produce your card unless you went through one of their photographers for a photoshoot. Well for the photoshoot, they required at least three clothing changes with hair and makeup professionally done for each change.

Basically, I had to pay to play, pay to get a job that offered payment. I spent more money to get a modeling portfolio and cards, just to walk in the agency office and see my modeling cards placed at the bottom of the model wall. The model wall is similar to a Wal-Mart grocery shelf, where you pay for your product placement on their shelf. Eye level, were the ones who got the paying jobs and I was at least bottom center, which amounted to nothing. They sent me unpaid job requests to an inactive email address I had asked them several times to remove from their database and then argued with me when I didn't respond in an hour to the email I didn't receive. In retrospect, I went from an illegitimate sham to a legitimate sham. One cost me dignity and the other time and money, no matter the route I got scammed either way.

The freelance photographer meant well, he was just trying to live out his dream but he had no plan and never delivered on a paycheck or any pictures for me to build my own portfolio in exchange for my time, which he had agreed. Needless to say, my big modeling dreams kept getting shut down and I settled with the fact that maybe it just wasn't for me. This wasn't the price I was willing to pay for wealth. I'd have to make it another way. The Circus job was not in the plan but at least I received regular payment for my time, which paid the bills, and my dignity wasn't at stake... just my sanity.

Working for The Circus resulted in being the foundation of who I am today but it wasn't without struggle for equality. The Ringmaster looked out for me for sure but there were times when I had to fight for equal pay, respect, and my worth. I remember having to literally argue with The Ringmaster and the executive director, who I call Geppetto, for a raise. They both agreed a person in my position and my experience deserved to make more money but because I was in my 20's, they flat out said I didn't deserve to make the salary associated with the work I was doing.

This type of discrimination is unfortunately common in almost every industry. The most harsh inequalities women face in the workplace are in promotion and compensation. Most of the time this type of discrimination is covert and embedded in HR policies stemmed in organizational structures and cultures. However, for executive leadership to sit me down in the office and candidly discuss their antiquated sexist views, was a hard pill to swallow. I'm glad they were honest about it but I was incredibly disturbed they justified these oppressive thoughts in a favorable tone as if they were helping me out.

In a separate conversation about how much money I wanted to make in general for any job in the future, I said I wanted to get to the point to make $150,000 a year, whether it was teaching or working for a corporation. They both tried their hardest to convince me I did not need that much money as a young woman and that I needed to make just enough to pay my bills and go on a few trips, they even proceeded to tell me I didn't need to travel as much as I had aspired. This coming from two men who made, from their current job, between $180,000-$200,000 annually. I was baffled at how when they spoke to male staff, interns, and young professionals affiliated with the company and they encouraged them to make as much money as possible but as a woman, they told me the opposite. I could not believe the hypocrisy in an organization where knowledge is power and an institution that prides itself on equipping Blacks for equal opportunities in the workplace. This was further demonstration of how the gender wage gap is perpetuated due to the personal biases of decision makers and why the environment was generationally toxic.

My conversations with them only proved to me how much of a burden we as racially minority women take on. We not only have to fight systemic governance because of the color of our skin but even have to fight within our own culture, fathers of daughters and leaders who have survived discriminatory practices themselves, in order for us to receive fair treatment.

I remembered being infuriated with them to the point of tears when I had to fight for a promotion I felt I had earned because I was given additional responsibilities of another position but not the pay nor the title. They told me I was too young to hold a director position and if they gave me the position, the older ladies on staff would be angry. I asked if they had reservations about my ability to do the job, they said 'no'. I asked if there was any other staff member capable of holding that position, they said 'no'. I asked what was the reason, and they confirmed it was my age and the fact the older ladies would be unhappy and think it was unfair.

I encourage you to clearly understand that toxicity occurs in the minds and personal views of individuals who look like you and claim to be on your side. If you recall, I told you people are fine with you as long as you stay in the box they have created for you. Without a doubt The Ringmaster and Geppetto looked out for me and supported me throughout my time at The Circus; however, there will never be a reason good enough to convince me their sexist beliefs weren't antebellum, discriminatory, and foul. Never lose sight of your dreams, do not negotiate your worth, and understand no one is above toxicity, so don't accept it.

Scammers

One thing I learned through all of my experiences in life is that scammers can come in any package. Growing up, I had only encountered a few professional scammers in the form of my cousins and close friends to the family. Their con was consistent: insurance fraud, slip and falls, petty theft, government service cons, etc., basically anything to not maintain a 9-5 but get a monthly check. I remember hearing family tell stories about how such and such was in jail as a result of their con and even heard adventures from the cons themselves about their latest petty heist. As a kid I found their stories amusing because it was full of excitement, mystery, and danger, just like television.

Their storylines were real adventures intertwined with fantasy, humor and tangible consequences. They were charismatic in every way. People enjoyed being around them because there was never a dull moment but hesitated to associate themselves with them in the general public to protect their own reputation. They understood it because it was part of the game; they knew who they were and didn't try to hide it. From my familial experience, I thought con artists were few and far between, but The Circus showed me they were a lot more common than I could have imagined.

When I moved away from home, I had no idea con artists would be so bold as to scam organizations and perpetrate themselves as educators and professionals. I know, you're saying, "duh, that is what a con artist does", but I guess I was limiting their capacity based on my experience. I learned there are various levels of this con game and its artists come in diverse forms but one thing they have in common, the one thing that unites them all, is desperation.

A Mountain Out of a Mole-Heel

After my personal experiences with Conny and Shaydee, I would encounter a few more cons as some temporary acts at The Circus. One I will never forget was a scammer in the least likely form, whom I will refer to as Ms. Heely. Ms. Heely was beautiful. She had long brown hair, a curvaceous shape, professional demeanor, with a calm and soothing voice. For most men over the age of 50, she was a knockout, as she was a good-looking lady in her early 50's. She had recently been hired in the executive office as a consultant to help with employee relations. She labeled herself as a "strategist" and seemed to have the resume, network, and experience to back it up.

The Ringmaster met her at one of the president's executive meetings and was somehow convinced she would be the solution to our department's staff relation problems. A sucker is born every minute and normally con artists can spot them in a crowd and she locked eyes on The Ringmaster. I remember him telling me about this impressive lady who was intelligent, charismatic, and professional who he thought would be a great mentor for me. He raved about how he believed she could be "the one" to turn our staff around and somehow magically get us to kumbaya, unlike the other consultants who talked a good game, got the first paycheck and disappeared into the thin air before performing any work.

The Ringmaster alerted me that he had finally invited Ms. Heely to come to the office to share ideas on how to improve employee relations through a series of meetings. Well, I was all in because he had always spoken highly of her. However, the moment she walked into the office and I laid eyes on her, I shook my head and knew it wasn't going to work.

Judging a book by its cover wasn't my MO but experience sometimes gives you answers to questions you don't have to ask. Like I said, there had been a recent influx of cons who had crossed a path a time or two, so if it walks and talks like a duck...it's a duck. The immediate thought that ran through my head was *how much money does she want?* It was evident to me The Ringmaster had just been suckered again. Danille and I had been down this road so many times, people talked a good game and The Ringmaster believed it and the next thing he invited them to the office only for us to have to deal with the aftermath of their destruction. Ms. Heely was nice but I knew with the older ladies we had in our department, they were not going to listen to this woman, she was too pretty and they would be too jealous.

Pretty discrimination or lookism is a real concept defined as prejudices someone has, strictly based on the appearance of others. Lookism is based on the physical stereotypes associated with one's appearance and how it is enacted through biases and discriminatory practices, whether it's positive or negative. A common dichotomy of this concept is how physically attractive people are perceived to be more economically valuable but not perceived as competent because of their looks. For women, this is very common as a pretty woman is more likely to have higher earnings than an unattractive woman but faces greater discriminatory practices than women with the same high status who are considered to have average to below average looks.

Under The Ringmaster's discretion, I prepped Ms. Heely for the personalities she would soon be responsible for transforming. She came to be aware of her surroundings and approached the ladies from a different angle; she made it clear she wasn't on The Ringmaster's side. Well she was nearly elected mayor as The Ringmaster was the most hated person among the staff. Anyone who was not an ally to him was a friend of theirs. They opened up, somewhat, to her during her one-on-one meetings with staff.

At first, Ms. Heely seemed to disprove my theory for the first couple of weeks, but she didn't even get to two months before she started exposing her true colors. First, she started canceling meetings and then no-showing. This was a total regression because she had almost won the trust of the old lady gang and they were coming to meet with her notebooks in hand, ready to lay it out but she would call five minutes before a scheduled meeting or slightly after to say she wasn't coming. Secondly, we found out she was not working for the executive office and actually wanted a job from The Ringmaster. Unfortunately, as we suspected, he gave her a job complete with her own office in our suite.

Thirdly, the information she collected with the meetings she did have with various staff, she gave to me to handle, while she collected a hefty consultant paycheck. The worst part was The Ringmaster had also supplied her with a laptop to conduct her work and administrative support through myself and other office staff. Here we go again, we thought, as we had seen several times this same story and its unfortunate ending. Danille and my thoughts were: *Why does he keep getting caught up with these con artists? This lady is faking!* All she had done in three months was meet with people during her first couple of weeks. There was no progression beyond that, no follow-up meetings, no written plans that she had promised to do. She basically fit into The Circus earning her reputation as a tightrope walker because of her ability to manipulate objects. In this case, our office and her employee relations skills were the objects of her manipulation.

She was always late and would sometimes have to reschedule meetings with The Ringmaster. Her consistent reason was being caught in traffic as to why she had to cancel and/or reschedule. Danille and I found this humorous because we knew she didn't have an office. The address she provided for an office was non-existent. After trying to track her down when she was late for meetings, we tried to reach her office only to discover it did not exist. The worst part was that we would later find out she didn't even have a home.

A damsel in despair, Ms. Heely caught the eye of Geppetto and he began to defend her once The Ringmaster had begun to realize Ms. Heely wasn't performing. It was a true lesson for us young women to see the softer side of men, how they cave at the sight of a beautiful woman, it was just ridiculous. Here was this nice lady, so we thought, until she started showing the usual signs of con artistry. When she started to ask us to do things for her, that is when Danille and I backed off and established a strictly cordial relationship of "hi" and "bye" greetings with her.

In short, Ms. Heely was a non-performing act who joined The Circus while passing by. She was receiving a consulting contract to improve employee relations in our department but she had missed and canceled meetings and not delivered a single recommendation or solution and now was saying she did not have a computer to complete her work. You can only imagine what happened next...The Ringmaster gave her a laptop that one of the other staff members had requested to use. How does a consultant who has their "own office" and "clients" not have a computer?

That's not all folks, Ms. Heely had another trick up her sleeve. With fake tears in her eyes, she told how the continuous breakdown of her car prevented her from meeting with her "clients"; thus, causing her to lose business. Feeling sorry for her, Geppetto lent her one of his vehicles, a PT Cruiser, to drive for free with the only responsibility to pay for her gas usage, which she later said she couldn't afford. He remarkably gave her gas money too.

As she continued to walk a tightrope, our complaints about her non-performance on her consultancy fell on deaf ears. The Ringmaster rebutted that we needed to be generous and help her through her hard times, so we would continue to pay her in exchange for using our resources and not fulfilling her contract. But yet I was told I could not have a raise for the work I was actually performing well. This was hard to digest, especially when Danille and I were left doing her work (note: she had a higher salary than ours) and when we asked for raises to compensate for our continuous additionally assigned duties, we were met with full opposition.

This situation was disappointing because the entire department had such high hopes for change, through her expertise, in the beginning and was shocked to see the layers unfold to yet another selfish scam. I cannot remember all of the antics that resulted in her employment there, as it was in excess. In summation, The Ringmaster's newly gained credibility plummeted even farther among the staff because this became another reason for them not to trust his judgment. He actually believed in her capabilities even after the facade vanished. Ms. Heely initially had a good talk, she had a lot of people fooled even after she had not followed through previously. There were events planned that others had to take over because she did not complete the work; these events involved community and corporate partners.

What happened was Ms. Heely went AWOL (absent without leave) and with the PT Cruiser. She had stopped coming to the office, stopped pretending to do work, and would not return phone calls or emails. In her absence, we unlocked her office to discover she had taken the laptop among other things that were in the office prior to her occupancy. Eventually, we had to stop her contract and send her emails threatening to press charges if she did not return the property (the property was paid with federal grant money given to the department which equals a federal offense) she took from the office she occupied.

Geppetto was so concerned because he had already had to get the PT Cruiser out of the impound because she had let her son drive it and he had accumulated a large amount of unpaid tickets. I had warned Geppetto to ask for his car back prior to the impound because when going to my car, I saw the PT Cruiser parked outside with her son in the driver's seat and piles of junk in the front passenger and back seats. It looked like someone was living out of the car. Geppetto did not listen and after weeks of hunting her down, he finally got the car back (it was in terrible condition) and we were finally rid of her and her antics.

One of the funniest things I will never forget about my experience with her was when I was in The Ringmaster's office on the couch that faced his desk. *A seat I notoriously occupied for observation purposes.* Ms. Heely was sitting in one of the chairs directly in front of his desk. The two of them were talking and I happened to glance down and notice her two-inch heeled, black sling backs. The heels on the shoes were destroyed. You could see the gray balls as the faux leather on the heel had peeled upward. Then I quickly realized the shoe heels were not the only heels in need of repair. The heels on her feet were in the worst shape I had ever seen in my life. They were ashy gray, as having a tremendous amount of dead skin on them, as if she had painted them a shade of cement gray. Then there was a rigiddly-shaped rectangular section on the side of her heel that had peeled and broken open with blood still in the gash. It was like a still river of blood with the peeling dead skin open, dubbing as the river bank surrounding the blood from the gray ash. Yes the ash was gray like ashes. In a state of unbelief, I had to excuse myself from the meeting and rush to get confirmation on the site I had just seen. Danille came into the office under the pretense to get The Ringmaster's signature, in order to see the unbelievable. I remember we laughed so hard at her heels that we cried. How could she let it get that bad? It was at that point we realized how bad off this woman was and this was beyond her being a scammer, this lady had real mental and hygiene problems.

Discrimination takes many forms and I have experienced it in ways unprotected by the law at the hands of people who were on my side. You can fight the powers of systematic oppression but what do you do when you are mistreated based on your youthful and attractive appearance? The moral laws are intangible and subjective, which means there is no enforcement. I'm sure through your various experiences you have come head on with discriminatory and unfair treatments based on factors unprotected by the law. These prime examples of the dynamic of toxic environments seem never ending. Regardless, you have to believe in yourself and keep going. The toxicity can come in many forms, so learn from this lesson that image is everything and use it to your advantage.

6   IT IS ALL IN A NAME

Nicknames, we all have had one and definitely have given them to someone whether they were aware or not. Sometimes nicknames are used to shorten someone's name, used as a term of endearment to describe an overshadowing personality or characteristic, or as a code so outsiders don't know who you are talking about (like what I'm alluding to). As a kid, we had nicknames growing up given to us by our family, like I was called Poe as a shortened version of my name. I had a cousin called Fats because he was a fat baby and I have an entire set of family members who I only knew by their nicknames, like Tootie, PeeWee, BeBe (pronounced Bay-Bay), Tiny, etc. I was an adult before I realized that Tootie's real name was Mae, Bebe's was Esther, PeeWee's was Cora, and I still don't know Tiny's. Well, I take that back, I knew Bebe's was Esther in my tweens when I saw her hit someone for calling her BeBe in front of a boy she liked.

We encountered nicknames not only from the familial environment but through our scholastic experiences too. These however seemed to be more descriptive in nature in order to distinguish, compare, or frankly, to label someone. I remember referring to someone as Stinky Eddy, so not to be confused with all the other Eddys I knew (who didn't smell like cat pee) because last names weren't known. When you are accepted into a sorority or fraternity, you earn or select your nickname, which is often called your line name to distinguish your personality among the group or reference characteristics from your initiation process. I could go on and on and so could you about all the subtle nicknames from high school. We even gave them to athletes based on their performance, which translated into the professional realm. Nicknames like: The Juice, Black Mamba, Air Jordan, King James, Big Papi, Mailman, The Answer, Prime Time, The Refrigerator, The Great One, and one of my favorites, Vinnie "The Microwave" Johnson, because he could score points in a short amount of time from off the bench.

The point is that nicknames are earned and like some early century cultures are a right of passage. Sometimes nicknames mean more to a person and say more about a person than their actual name. They describe us and motivate us. Think about how Muhammed Ali coined himself as "The Greatest" and he is still, arguably, the greatest boxer of all time. What I'm saying is we tend to live up to our nicknames until we prove them invalid or simply outgrow them.

Well nicknames are given on the job too. Similar to the professional athlete nicknames, work nicknames are based on performance or a distinguishing characteristic. Unlike the athlete names, sometimes the work nicknames are given in secrecy because you are being talked about on a regular basis and not because your colleagues think the world of you.

A Floral Arrangement

This chapter is dedicated to a woman, who my coworkers and I referred to as "Floral". To her face and in public conversations we referred to her as Ms. and her last name. But when she walked out of our office suite, she was Floral. Why such a pleasant name you ask? Because she notoriously wore the same floral sweater...every week....sometimes consecutive days. It wasn't an outerwear type of sweater. How she earned the name, sort of went like this: She walks into the office without speaking and goes directly to Mr. Bailey's office (with whom she had an on and off again romantic relationship). She would often come to his office every time something didn't go her way to complain. One day, in one of her frantic rants, she came in and stomped out and the comment was made, "if she comes in here one more time with that floral sweater" and someone added "didn't she wear that sweater yesterday and last week but she's always at the mall buying clothes though". Then on another day a commotion was heard in the front part of the office and someone asked who it was and the response was "Floral"...and the rest became office history.

Ironically, Floral was a colorful character with quite the arrangement. There were days and ways in which she blossomed and then there was...well when she didn't, to say the least. When meeting her during my first days of working at The Circus, she was pleasant. She immediately sparked conversation with me, stating the reason for her draw to me was that I reminded her of her daughter, because we were the same age. Additionally, Floral and I were sorority sisters so we had a common bond. She'd come to the office to have brief lighthearted talks with me and would often extend a helping hand, if I needed it. I thought she was friendly plus I would also see her in the mall on the weekends frequently because we both loved to shop.

As our work relationship bloomed, my supervisor mentioned to me, one day after she saw Floral leaving my office, to watch out for her. I quickly realized no one in the office had any interaction with her except for Mr. Bailey. As time evolved, then I noticed that anytime something needed to be communicated to Floral from my office, my supervisor would nominate me to tell her stating "That's Porscha's sorority sister, let her tell her. They're friends. She hates the rest of us". This was a common phrase and always said in the cadence of an elementary-aged instigator. Young and unbothered, I gladly accepted it because Floral had never done anything harmful to me and I had no evidence of the awful things they said about her.

After a few months of working there, I finally accepted Floral's offer to visit her office. I really didn't go in there with the sole intention of striking a conversation with a woman my mother's age as a girl in my early 20's, but by popular office vote, found myself in her office to deliver a message and package. That's when I noticed her office was different from any others I had seen; it was cluttered. A mountain range of paper lined her desk and wall with peaks and valleys of loose leaf paper. A variety of colored folders were scattered around the office like confetti and opened boxes, knick knacks, and paddy whacks took residence in every empty space. I was stunned.

Happy to see me, she grinned from ear to ear and invited me to sit so we could talk. I said I'd stand because sitting on the papers and magazines in her guest chairs wasn't my idea of hospitality. Little did I know that she would hold me hostage for an hour rambling about how much she hated the people in my office and why they were "snakes" and I should watch my back. Immediately, I began to see my positive outlook on my work environment deteriorate because now I was being brought into the drama, a place I did not want to be because this meant I would soon have to choose a side. The fact is, I didn't want to be on a side, I just wanted to do my work in peace, eat free food every chance I got and go home at 5pm sharp, and earn my paycheck.

Sad to say, the characteristics my office had pre-warned me about Floral slowly began to surface. It was over a period of time with gradual leaks until one day the lid just came all the way off the cup, never to be sealed again. I cannot pinpoint the actual moment where I realized I could not stand her and that the sight of her made me want to sigh, but I reached the same sentiment of the rest of the office, which was just not wanting to communicate with her at all, because it was exhausting and pointless.

After that fateful day of being in her office, I learned to keep my conversations with her short and sweet. I still thought she was a good person because she hadn't done anything to ME that would make me feel otherwise. Besides, we're in a work environment and to be professional and cordial was my goal. There were times where remaining neutral felt more like being a wishbone. However, I remained neutral and gave diplomatic answers when either party spoke ill of the other or when they tried to see where my loyalty resided. Truth be told, both sides got on my nerves and outside of work, I wouldn't associate with either, but of course I wouldn't share how I really felt to either of them.

One day the paint started to peel. I saw how Floral would do extreme measures and would flat out call someone a liar in their face in front of guests as if to embarrass them, when it actually embarrassed her and our department. Throughout this all, I kept smiling and shortening our already short talks in an effort not to be sucked into the negativity. Through these little shenanigans here and there, too many to remember, I began to feel sorry for her because I noticed there was a more significant problem than her not getting along with others. Recognizing this, being as selfish as I am with my food, when she asked me for a can of tuna to eat because she forgot her lunch, I gave it to her. The funny thing was, I noticed she tended to "forget" her lunch often and each time she asked, I gave it to her, though she had worn out her welcome. I just felt sorry for her because I felt there was something deeper happening in her life.

My sympathy was soon short lived when we had an argument over how much of my food she thought I should give her. The debacle was petty on the surface; however, there was a significant underlying principle of respect that was being violated. Once this happened, I realized she had not forgotten her lunch all those times, she was in some weird and twisted way trying to exercise control over me.

The story goes, I was sitting down eating fried shrimp out of a styrofoam take-out box that my favorite co-worker/friend, Danille, and I had just purchased. Now during that time in my life, shrimp and I were best friends and there was nothing that could come between us. Not even the pity of an old hungry woman who no one seemed to like. Floral had previously walked into the office suite and was in Mr. Bailey's office. After being in there for a while, she comes to where we are eating to say hello; however, I had a huge problem with how she decided to deliver her greetings. She came and stood directly in front of me as if she was trying to tower over me, which immediately caused me to feel uncomfortable. She then began to ask questions about what I was eating. I said "shrimp" and as soon as I said the obvious to any seeing person, she reached over my plate and attempted to take a shrimp off of my plate. My body temperature began to rise because for one, I was tired of her always asking me for my food, 2) I didn't like how she was standing over me, and 3) it is never okay to reach onto someone's plate without permission.

My natural reaction was to cover my food as if I was trying to shield it from harm. She said, "you're not going to give me a shrimp". I responded, "I only have 6". She then looked at my co-worker as if to see if she was watching. She continued, "Give me a shrimp" with a playful yet uncomfortable laughter.

-"No!"

-"You're not going to give me a shrimp? You got more, just give me one."

-"No, I only have six."

-"Whaat! After all I've done for you?" as she looks at Danille who is giving a look of fear in anticipation of what is to come.

I responded, "All you've done for me? All you've done for me? Please, didn't I always give you tuna and bread when you asked me? I don't owe you nuthin!"

-"Oh I haven't done nothing for you? Give me a shrimp!"

I continued to eat my shrimp while trying to calm myself and not show the same disrespect that I felt she had shown me.

She continued, "Oh it's like that, you gonna do me like that. I'll remember that next time you need me."

-"Remember it, I don't care. I'll remember that the next time you come begging me for some tuna. The next time I need you? Please, you ain't done nothing for me."

As she begins to walk out of the office repeating "Uh-huh, I'll remember that."

This interaction would not be the last but is the shift that ultimately changed our relationship because all of the animosity I had toward her had been revealed in that three minute moment. I no longer had to choose a side or play the fence. She no longer had to demonstrate that I was on her side because it was now clear, I was not. When situations like this arise, you always have to look at what's underneath the surface, what caused the altercation, why did this conflict happen. With problems like this brewing in the workplace, you have to begin to address it at the beginning, the root; otherwise, it escalates and infects the thoughts of others.

Before the *shrimp gate*, I saw the extent of her hatred for some of the folks in my office which concerned me and became the ultimate proof I could no longer be around her energy. My interactions with her became short and were strictly about the job.

One weekend, when the building was closed in the early hours of the morning, a current employee, high on drugs (according to the building security), broke into the building and went on a fit of destruction. He ripped projectors from the ceiling and stole computer equipment among other things and stashed them in his apartment across the street. In the process, he used a crowbar to break into several offices, ransacking some. Among those completely damaged were the Ringmaster's, Bobbi's, and the IT director 's (his supervisor), which not only had things stolen but had broken glass and other items and drawers ripped out. The destruction was so severe, the police who caught him in the act stated that had someone been in the building while he was there, they would have been dead. He was a small guy, 5'10, 165 lbs and it took multiple police officers to restrain him because of the strength he had from the drugs.

Knowing the severity of this issue, the morning all staff returned to the office, I went to Floral's to record any damage her office may have experienced. It was at that point I saw her true colors. She began to talk about how the three offices that had been hit the worst, deserved it and how the damage should have served as a wake up call to the individual office occupants. I reminded her that breaking into a building is a crime and then destroying offices and stealing equipment from the building we were in was a federal crime and how we all should be thankful no one was harmed in the process.

She continued to go on about how if the persons were in their offices at the time he was on his path of destruction, she would not have cared. It was then I realized how much she hated the Ringmaster and Bobbi. For me, humanity would have kicked in, no matter how I felt about a person. I would hope you wouldn't want someone harmed who has not done any physical or emotional harm to you. I know I wouldn't, hate doesn't run that deep in my veins but apparently it did for her. I commented twice to see if she was just venting but she wasn't, she meant what she said and never wavered from it, even days after the incident. That is when I knew she had to be handled with care.

And the Beat Goes On

The years would continue with her antics not only displayed towards me but others in my office. It came to the point where Mr. Bailey even stated she 'was out of control' and didn't want to have any dealings with her. So what do you do when confrontation is inevitable? It was hard for me to face this everyday and have to work with a person who was unstable and had developed a complex that everyone was against her. In her mind, she felt certain people wanted her job. Anytime you had to ask her a question(s) you primarily had to walk on eggshells or if she submitted something and it was wrong, it took two days to rehearse how you were going to deliver the news because you knew, no matter what, there was a 90% chance she would not receive the information and turn a regular conversation into a full-blown argument. It was so uncomfortable and unproductive.

It was not a coincidence in her behavior as it was made clear to me later on that she was suffering from the paranoid personality disorder. The constant suspicion others were trying to sabotage her or were after her job and the overall odd behavior were prime characteristics of this disorder. Cluster A is a designation of the personality disorder where other symptoms, such as always being on guard, thinking others are seeking to demean or bring them harm, are normally unfounded beliefs they harbor that prevent them from forming positive relationships and having productive interactions with colleagues. When you come across this type of coworker, know they are often argumentative, distrustful of everyone, unforgiving, extremely sensitive, stubborn, and ignorant of their role in office conflicts. They also perceive there are hidden meanings in common and/or innocent remarks, react in anger through retaliatory efforts, and take criticism as an attack. Most of the time, people display the majority of the symptoms related to this disorder but Floral demonstrated all.

There are several stories of encounters with her but the ones I remember were in a meeting of about 10 people and the discussion was about the

70

recruitment and marketing of a program. She came into the meeting with a stack of papers stating she was "about to prove her case". I remember the look of confusion on everyone's face as if they had just walked into the Twilight Zone, trying to scramble what "case" she was referring to and why there was a "case" to begin with. The meeting begins and The Ringmaster shares with the room a customer complaint about a document that had not been submitted on their behalf by the program coordinator, which was Floral. She sharply interrupts the meeting and forcibly slides paper across the table at myself and another person to show us proof of a conversation she had with someone. She failed to understand no one had questioned her conversation, rather it was the lack of her submission of the client's document that had caused a problem, ergo the purpose of the meeting. When she shoved one of the sheets across the table, it almost gave a paper cut to the other person, as the paper flew up during the slide, nearly grazing their head.

Chalking this experience up to another one of her antics, I remained nonchalant as I did hakuna matata to myself and repeated in my brain "it's me, not her". I had to take the burden of responsibility to not upset her and not to react to her antics because it was just another demonstration of her instability and her way of trying to force a negative reaction. The high road was the only one I was on. However, me and my high road seemed to bother her as she received no confrontation when she slid those papers. In fact, I didn't even pick up or touch the papers and made no comment about the inappropriateness of her sliding them.

Now she was angry because she was perceived from those in attendance as being aggressive. After the conclusion of the meeting, I went to Danille's office to discuss payroll and suddenly Floral appeared just outside of the door. I see her out of my peripheral vision but continue with my conversation without acknowledging her presence. Still standing waiting to be noticed, my co-worker sees her and says underneath her breath "Why is she just standing there. Why doesn't she leave?" I responded, "I know. She just wants to start something that's why I'm not paying her any mind."

Then I guess Floral decided she was tired of being unnoticed, so she said "Oh, you're just going to ignore me?" I continued on with my conversation with Danille, when her voice elevated to a six out of 10 and she continued "You thought you got me in that meeting don't you? You tried to put me on blast in front of everybody." Aww, why did I break my silence, it was killing her softly so well. I just honestly thought she was crazy enough to stand there until Jesus came and since no one knows the day nor the hour when He will appear, I thought, 'let me just get this over with'. I responded, "Nobody put you on blast. I was asked what happened and I explained what happened. You put yourself on blast when you tried to overtalk The Ringmaster and he told you to hush. Then you threw paper at people once you realized how stupid you sounded...Now that was professional!"

She tried to refute and I said "I'm not talking about it anymore because I explained it to you many times before the meeting, trying to save your face but you had to keep going until you got shut down by The Ringmaster. So case closed!" as I swatted my hands like I was trying to shoo a fly. Then I went back to completing my conversation with Danille as Floral began to shout on and on about the situation. She just couldn't leave anything alone.

I know you have co-workers or even friends that just don't let anything die. The problem can be solved, dead, and buried and they still want to talk about it as if it is still relevant. The horse is dead, mutilated, buried, in fact we cremated it...can you stop talking about it? It's not coming back but yet they are still talking about it. They just won't let it go, so much has happened since then and it wasn't even that big of a deal in the first place and yet you are still talking about it. Yes, she was one of those and I kept letting her talk because there was no use.

The saying *don't argue with a fool because no one can tell the difference* helped me out a lot with dealing with people like her. What's the point? I remember Erykah Badu had a song that said, "What good do your words do if they can't understand you. Don't go talking that sh*t." Those were words to live by. *I can't explain it to you because you don't want to hear it.* I could say 'you know what, I agree with you' and she would still continue to argue, so that's when I realized I could not win by joining her. Whoever came up with the saying, *If you can't beat them, join them* didn't work with these types of people. Someone on Floral's level has every right to plead reason of insanity and I would absolutely lose, so in order to stay sane, I had to remember "It's me, not her".

It's literally my fault because I'm not crazy, so it is on me to make the decision on how to handle this situation in the most professional way. I should not have said anything to her besides, "I tried to explain it to you and you felt that wasn't good enough. I had no control of what happened in that meeting and I'm sorry you felt that I put you on blast, that was never my intention. I told my side and now I'm moving on and hope you can too." Then remove myself from the environment. Now she probably would not have received it and would have wanted to talk more but one thing that must be understood when dealing with these folks, just state the facts, look them in the eye, remain calm, and walk away. You have to adopt the spirit of being unbothered really because it's all foolishness and if that is not the energy you possess, then it doesn't have a home inside of you. Don't allow it to manifest in your environment; otherwise, it will become toxic.

How did this segment end, epically. Once I delivered the "case closed" line to her with the gesture of the gavel and the fly shoo, I finished my conversation and walked right past her, made no eye contact and went to my office. Danille got on her computer and Floral was left in the middle of the office with no one to argue with and the audience she thought she had, had gone when she started to raise her voice towards me. That is a lesson, you have to physically isolate them. Toxic individuals thrive off attention, positive or negative, so when you deprive them of that and deprive them of the reaction they want, they are left dangling. Just like she was in that meeting when she tried to goat me into a reaction and it didn't work, then she tried again and she got a little bit of traction, which was my fault. The bottomline is you cannot expect these people to change, you have to change, meaning change how you deal with them.

The shenanigans just didn't stop there, she just moved to another target. She did try once to rekindle our flame per se, but I just walked off and she left me alone. The incident happened a quick minute when I came into the main area of the office suite to get a document from her that she was bringing to me because I didn't want her in my personal office. As I came around the corner, she dropped to her knees as if she was worshiping and handed me the paper and then began to loudly proclaim me as royalty saying "Here you go oh queen" as she continued to bow. I got the paper before that face of hers hit the floor to complete the first bow and I went back to my office. No eye contact. I don't know how long she continued being the court jester and frankly didn't care either, because like I said, I left. I heard from the office receptionist that there were other people in the office at the time looking at her strangely and she got up giggling and left talking outloud.

That was the last time I had to directly deal with her before she started with other folks in my office. I soon informed them of the "It's me, not them" theory. I must admit it was hard for them to accept that you have to hold yourself accountable for your actions with the toxic and release them of all responsibility for behaving insanely in the situation. The staff wanted to give her a piece of their mind but they soon began to realize that it resulted in nothing. It didn't make a difference and if someone walked in, they could clearly argue that they didn't know who was the sane person.

Collectively, we were able to shield ourselves from her antics and she spent less and less time in our suite. She didn't change at all, she just took her antics elsewhere and that was fine just as long as my staff didn't have to deal with her shenanigans. I must mention that her last stab at our office was with the office receptionist, who was the last to adopt the "It's me, not them" philosophy. This was probably, hands down, the most ludicrous thing I've heard of and it was her last and yet sad play to harass someone in our office. There is no way to really set this up and it is no lie, you just can't make this up.

Foldergate

One day, the office receptionist receives a call from building security with notification they are investigating a theft case filed against her by Floral. Astonished, she asked what was stolen and the officer said...*drum roll please...*"a blue folder". Yes folks, Floral went through the trouble and time and effort to actually file a theft report of a blue file folder stating the receptionist took it from her office. The contents of the folder still remains a mystery; there was no real description of what was in the folder except that the contents were confidential and vital to Floral's job.

I told you previously her office was the equivalent of the aftermath of a Midwest tornado, but for some reason, she thought the receptionist went to her office to steal a folder…not her purse, picture frame, but a blue folder. Floral went as far as to send emails to others in the workplace labeling the receptionist as a thief because of the case of the missing file folder. It was pretty bad and ridiculous. After months of animosity between the two, the case was dismissed when Floral's assistant found the folder in question in Floral's office under a pile.

Watts in a Name

When we had a new office receptionist, Floral would do her same move to befriend her and then begin to talk about how everyone in our office was against her and wanted her job. The script remains the same, once folks truly experience her, the good and then the real side, they pull away and then she begins to attack them, as she did with me, the office receptionist (from Foldergate), and the others. It starts off with little things here and there and then it just gets out of hand and you seriously question her maturity. I was no longer amazed at her antics after the blue foldergate. She could not do anything after that to shock me anymore.

I do remember there being a confrontation with the new receptionist because Floral accused her of not responding to "important" emails but the receptionist continuously stated she never received such emails. As usual, Floral came with a stack of printed emails claiming the receptionist had been unresponsive to the emails she sent. The receptionist recognized from the stack of "evidence", Floral had actually sent these emails in question to someone else with the same first name but different last name. The receptionist tried multiple times to explain this to her with no resolve. Floral then began to argue for months about how the receptionist's last name was Watts, despite the receptionist constantly repeating her last name was not Watts, in fact it had never been Watts, but according to Floral, that was her name. It was a Twilight Zone moment.

On to the Next One

Floral did not run out of targets or people to accuse in her paranoia. She had run-ins with the others outside of our department, such as the finance department's assistant director (AD) because Floral had refused to enter information via the online system. She would instead send emails for this AD to input though she was in charge of entering the payees for our specific department. In lieu of learning how to key in the information, Floral continued to send emails and copy at least six people on the email to show she was "doing her job" since she had now joined the chorus of Tupac Shakur's *Me Against the World* song.

She's excessive in sending emails, because again, she is trying to show people she is working but all she is really doing is showing how she is competing for the Guinness World Records as the most annoying person sending the most emails about the same subject in one day. I think one time, I counted 15 emails in a thread she sent about the same thing giving play by play of three phone calls she made and who she talked to in response to an issue that was on hold until further information from a donor. In the email, she copied everyone from multiple offices and unrelated departments.

The most ridiculous example of the serial email copier was when the building manager sent an email to The Ringmaster and copied Geppetto and Floral describing an incident of how Floral hosted a membership drive equipped with a microphone in the lobby of the building while meetings were taking place. What was Floral's response? She forwarded the email with the message of "Consider yourselves warned." and who did that email go to?...a whopping 164 people. The irony was she took offense for months because I expressed that I felt her way of communication was unprofessional; however, she succeeded at proving me right.

The Lesson

People with the paranoid personality disorder often get this way by overcoming a traumatic physical or emotional experience in their personal life or some pivotal experience rooted in the organization's culture before you came along. Effective communication in the clarity of your factual statements in response to their perspective is key to dealing with the people who have this disorder. The biggest lesson to learn from toxic individuals like Floral, who go above and beyond to pollute the work environment, is to ignore them. Obey the signs at The Circus and don't feed the animals. If you do, you have just lost the battle. You have to take the high road at all costs and eventually, they will move on to another target. The moral of this story, do not waste your energy, be kind and move on because you have greater things ahead.

7   THE TRUTH ABOUT LOCUSTS

God created multiple creatures of all shapes and sizes, each to perform a specific task on the earth. As such, each one of us as human beings has a purpose and it is our choice whether we fulfill that calling or we select a different path for ourselves. I respect God as the creator of all things though I question the existence of some of the creations, like a gnat, fly, snake, locust, etc. Is there such a purpose to annoy, frighten, kill or destroy? If so, then can we actually love God yet hate his creation for doing its devine role? Maybe it's that we never understand the specific purpose of everything but we accept that it has a purpose. Sometimes, maybe sometimes, that misunderstood purpose, in the long run, benefits us in some odd way if we stick to our purpose. The irony is some humans' behavior can be likened to these "unpurposeful" creatures and then the question still remains in my mind, what purpose do they serve?

Let's take the locust for instance. A locust by definition is a breed of a grasshopper, often known to destroy vegetation and symbolize a plague. This could not be a better description of a few people who hopped their way into our lives at The Circus. We had our share of folks pretending to be consultants to help our department not fall into the depths of destruction that was the generational culture of the entire organization. However, none fared to be the change agent they promoted themselves to be but actually equated to be yet another advocate of the cursed culture we were trying to be rescued from. What was their purpose?

Sociality and Survival

This one time, not like the others, we thought we had found "the one" or rather she had found us and would lead our department from going down the road of traditional despair. Liesa was her name. She was a consultant to whom The Ringmaster had been introduced by an acquaintance. She was this sweet, late 30's looking woman with orangish-red hair, like fire, who was friendly, polite, and efficient. She was very business-oriented and genuinely seemed like she wanted to help us grow. Immediately, she recognized our promotional materials were weak and offered to help with the rebranding. When we needed something, she did it. She had the graphic capabilities we lacked and she could do it quickly and her attitude was very positive, so she gained our trust. We appreciated working with someone who didn't prove to be a product of this wicked culture we bathed in Monday through Friday.

Like much of the others who had entered our doors, Liesa also came alone but differed as she had no previous ties or experience with the organization. It is known for species of grasshoppers to have different exterior patterns or colors to designate their origin. A solitary creature with short horns, locusts prefer to exist daily on their own unless they are faced in a challenging situation, to where they use sociality as a survival mechanism. As such, I don't know what Liesa's situation was prior to coming to our office, but she became highly socialized in our environment. She was a small business owner who led on to be a one woman show, which was one of the reasons she promised to work hard for us and a reason The Ringmaster gave her a chance. He felt like he was helping a lady to grow her business, which made sense because we were committed to providing practical business education and helping historically marginalized individuals and communities.

The Swarming Phase

Distinguishing itself from other forms of grasshoppers, locusts are harmless alone but have the ability to swarm if in an intermittent situation. Liesa and her one-woman show started off completing ad-hoc small jobs and after being duped by several crooks before, we, as an entire department, found her refreshing. Liesa was articulate and dressed professionally whenever she came to the building. She greeted everyone with a smile and asked about our day. What I appreciated most about her was she followed protocol for things to be done. When someone would try to backdoor me and have her do something, she would always bring it to me before starting the project, to ensure I had approved the need for the document and the content, as I was in charge of the branding. I'm sure it was also to make sure she got paid for each item she did, but either way, I appreciated the transparency. I liked her, Danille liked her and of course, The Ringmaster loved her. Even Floral was happy to have her aboard because she was pleasant and accommodating.

It was almost like she was a dream come true. Well, sometimes if it is too good to be true, more than likely it is but if you give it a good 90 days, the truth will often reveal itself, whether purposefully or not. It's hard for anybody to keep a facade that long without some of their true self seeping out. In a lengthier time than it took others, we would learn yet another long and hard lesson. For me, this would be my turning point; Liesa gave me a tutorial I would never forget which ended my time of learning things the hard way.

My time at The Circus had been eventful, to say the least, before the arrival of Liesa. I was blessed to experience a lot of great times with the forming of true friendships, learning the business network, gaining valuable work experience, and developing my professional skills. Up until this time, I thought my management skills had improved. Once Bobbi left, Medusa soon followed, leaving me to inherit all of the duties of a public relations director along with my current duties, which would result in a newly created position for my late twenties self.

In my new role, I needed help. We had a receptionist on staff that was dubbed as the creative artist for the department; the only problem was her capabilities in this area plateaued in the early 90's and graphics had progressed since then. The rest of the departmental staff was constantly sending her requests for marketing materials and it was now my job to centralize this process and brand our department as a viable competitor in the 21st century. Therefore, Liesa's arrival was like manna from heaven because she understood a new era of marketing was needed and it started with having current pictures and updated collateral.

Liesa to the rescue, was what many of us thought; it was as if she had spotted us and knew our needs before we asked them. However, there was one doubter in the group, Mrs. Charles, who's personality I could describe in one word...grumpy. Mrs. Grumpy was never fond of Liesa but on the other hand, she was not a fan of any woman. Not sure what the entire gender had ever done to one of our own to bring on such disdainful treatment but this time she recognized Liesa's game before it was played. I remember while all of us, the staff, were in awe at how great she was, Mrs. Grumpy was mean to her. Liesa would always ask why Grumpy was so mean and we would offer an apologetic statement, painting her out to be this uber banshee that she actually was. We should not have spoken of Grumpy in such a way, because she was an elder but we just wanted someone outside of us to see what we had endured for years. I initially thought the distaste was because Liesa was White and Grumpy was one of the old school Black women who, due to racial oppression, did not trust Whites. It was clear Grumpy's relational aggression and lookism was in full effect.

Liesa was endeared to us, almost as if she was family, that I almost fell out of my chair one day when The Ringmaster said she was of mixed-race. *Whaat!* I don't understand why people cannot be accepted in the form, shape, size, and color they are without being symbolically metamorphosed into the physical culture of the adopting party. When he said that Danille and I looked at each other like, "oh now she's Black?" He then went on to justify his statement by saying it was the reasoning behind her having an olive skin tone and not having blonde hair. A pretty ridiculous reach I thought, but I grew up in a predominantly White environment and I can assure anyone who hasn't, White people have other natural hair colors other than blonde and that doesn't make them Black. It was obvious to most that she was a natural redhead who had colored her hair which resulted in the unique fire color. When we weren't convinced by his reclamation of this quintessential racial passer, he referenced her having "full lips" and a Black husband as his closing argument.

It was hilarious and borderline pathetic because this woman had no typical physical features of a Black person and yet he was trying his hardest to convince that somehow Liesa had an allegiance to the Black culture as if it was a way to accept her or to justify her working with us. Needless to say, no one believed she was Black and could care less that she was White. I'm sure you were wondering if her husband was White; yes, and he possessed some racist and sexist undertones as we would later find out. To say we had some healthy laughter from The Ringmaster's rationalizations would be an understatement. Tears were forming as he kept grasping for straws to make this conviction that only he believed and found necessary. We looked at him so hard with the scrunchy face and laughed so hard that I think he was embarrassed to the point he wanted to kick us out of his office.

The Plague

As time went on, Liesa spent more and more time in the building to the point she was given her own office. In the months we had become accustomed to seeing her on a daily basis, her welcome soon started to wear off and folks began to see what Grumpy noticed at first sight. Ms. Billy, who was over the programming office, had eventually developed a dislike of Liesa simply because she felt she was a liar.. I valued Ms. Billy's wisdom, biased wisdom, but I valued it because she had been at The Circus for decades and was an ally to me. However, you always had to seek supporting documents because her perception of people was often based on the level of respect that she believed they had towards her . Ms. Billy wouldn't give specifics to why she believed Liesa was a liar but she did express how Liesa's choice of brochure pictures was not representative of our department..

It so happened, the more Liesa worked for us, her true self began to unravel. My naivety chalked it up to The Circus getting to her. The reality was Liesa's once innovative ideas and graphic abilities became the same innovative ideas and graphic abilities. All the flyers and printing documents she would do, were now replicas of what she previously had done. I would tell her the look and feel we wanted for a document and instead of doing what was requested, she'd make suggestions and then do it the way she wanted, which was the total opposite.

Disappointment began to settle in as Liesa was falling into the pattern of the con-artists of the past and present (because they always come back). She had started to have one-on-one meetings with The Ringmaster and from prior experience, that is a recipe for disaster. On top of that, she would slip in extra costs on the invoice that she did not perform; thus, losing favor with Danille and proving to be the untrustworthy person Ms. Billy had claimed her to be. She had basically turned me off when she attempted to teach me a lesson on a project that I had given her. For some odd reason, she behaved in a way as if she had hired us and not the other way around. One by one we gradually started to pull away from her as each of us experienced some portion of what Grumpy saw in the beginning. Her ability to meet deadlines dwindled and it was always followed up with some lame excuse, which eventually fully bloomed into multiple lies.

Things were changing as now the small talk we all once had with her turned into silence during passing. Depersonalization had set in as it was quickly becoming obvious her actions had resulted in people only wanting to deal with her regarding work matters, and some did not want to interact with her at all. She had been ostracized from the family as cordial interactions were only done on an as needed basis. As the effects of being an outsider kicked in, she would often lash out on the receptionist in our office by ordering her around and speaking to her sarcastically.

The Gregarious Phase

In the gregarious phase, locusts become cohesive in their movement, merging with other bands to survive, including helping each other to maneuver around barriers. Because they feel threatened, they will join forces to become more abundant. This is the time where their behavior and habits change due to new circumstances and as a cohesive unit, travel downhill resulting in a damage of vegetation and a cause of a plague.

The preliminary damage had already been done with the lies and disrespect she had shown the staff, but it was really just a taste of what was yet to come, especially for me. Liesa had lost the trust and camaraderie of the staff and had now infected The Ringmaster. Her contract was over and the news of it was like sweet music to our ears. However, The Ringmaster had already taken a bite from her apple and hired her for a full-time public relations position, reporting to me. This gave her a steady paycheck and solved the problem she had with not receiving benefits as an entrepreneur. He thought the entire staff was being mean to her for an unmerited reason. The fact was everyone, except Grumpy, had liked her up until now, so sometimes you have to check to see why the temperature changed, it just didn't happen on its own.

My grace towards Liesa ended when I received a response email from her that had some harsh words in the email thread. I am the one who reads the email in its entirety, even the previous emails in the thread because I always want to get a full understanding. In doing so, I just happened to read all the way down where she had sent an email to her husband, who was her invisible business partner. We would find out he was actually the artist behind all of the graphics she had done for us. Liesa was just the front person, the face of the business.

Anyway, her husband had responded in that email thread with a message that had racial undertones. I sat in my office to read over it a few times to confirm I didn't misunderstand or read too much into the email. Convinced and offended, I printed the email and took it to The Ringmaster for him to read it in its entirety. This was a pivotal moment as The Ringmaster would begin to see that Liesa wasn't all she had represented herself to be. This email had exposed Liesa as a liar and now The Ringmaster could see for himself the things she had told him in confidence was not only calculated but with malicious intent.

What had transpired was Liesa's husband, Marx, started sending me emails regarding the graphics (that's how Danille and I knew for sure it wasn't her making the graphics, as she had led on) and I noticed his grammar was horrific. This could have been one reason she kept him invisible because he wasn't socially savvy. However, as Liesa took on more work with us, she let the cat (husband) out of the bag, so I would now get emails from him regarding approvals of the final documents.

At first, I had no issue with Marx doing the graphics and no problem with working with him. I was disappointed Liesa felt it necessary to seek sympathy as a "one woman show", when she actually had a business partner the entire time. It was dishonest and then there was no introduction of Marx; it was just a surprise email to me from Marx for an approval of a document I had discussed with Liesa in totality. I felt the communications with Marx were a bit amateurish as if I was not dealing with a business professional though I found him to have professional knowledge of graphics that far exceeded Liesa's, so I understood the partnership.

Things had become complicated when Marx told me to copy him on all emails sent to Liesa. I thought it was strange because Liesa was now hired as a full-time employee and we had not hired Marx to do anything, so to copy him on company emails was out of protocol. In his defense, perhaps there was some miscommunication between the two of them, maybe Liesa hadn't told him she was hired as a regular employee and she was getting a monthly paycheck as an individual and not a consultant. Possibly, The Ringmaster could not have explained to her the difference between being a consultant versus an employee; however, I discussed it with her when she tried to give me assignments.

Prior to her full-time hiring, whenever I would receive communication (it was always via email) from Marx, it would contain numerous grammatical errors in the email explanation and the document proof. When I would provide changes to the proof he sent, he would display his anger at having to make changes and would in turn send me emails explaining why the proof should not be revised to reflect the grammatical change. This was weird because that is the purpose of the proof, to make changes and/or correct errors before finalizing the document. However, he felt I should accept whatever he created, right or wrong, on the premise that he was the expert. He became angrier with each correction. I mentioned to The Ringmaster how

I was almost to the point of not wanting to deal with him as our point of contact because our contract was with Liesa, not him. He also told me to provide my personal cell number so he could contact me for emergency printing.

The Ringmaster thought Marx' actions were weird but encouraged me to continue to deal with him as it would help Liesa to focus on other work she was hired to do. I continued as instructed until I received another aggressive email from Marx telling me to schedule a meeting with him and The Ringmaster, so he could explain to me how to manage the media. This was after he had requested a file approval from me that he claimed I did not send. However, it was a break in communication because I sent the file to Liesa and she didn't send it to him.

I replied to his email informing him I would no longer communicate with him. He was unaware that I had read the other emails in the thread he had sent to Liesa, where he spoke ill of our entire office. Marx was accusing me of not getting something in on time when his wife was the one who didn't do things on time and somehow had made him believe it was me holding things up. Plus, this was after Liesa had accepted the full time position. I replied to his email,

> "I gave the approval for the brochures on Monday,
> as noted in your email sent to Liesa at 12:43 am
> this morning. Thanks for your thoughts and gracious
> offer on media management. From now on, Liesa will
> be my contact, as at the end of the day, she's the one
> that is employed with The Circus. The Ringmaster's
> executive assistant will be happy to assist you with
> making an appointment."

Liesa and Marx irked me to no return. I agree couples should stick together, but this is business and to deal with both of them and the fact they didn't communicate with each other, was just too much for one to endure. The Ringmaster's executive assistant had issues with him as well sending rudely toned emails. One day, I decided to vent my frustrations with him via my aforementioned email. I corrected his grammar throughout the email thread and then highlighted them, so he would note the corrections. I had every intent to be sarcastic in letting him know he was busted talking about members of our office and since he had sent a prior email saying to highlight any changes in documents so he could find them easily, I obliged. I laughed as I typed and highlighted because I knew it would get under his skin, just like the very sight of his email address got under mine. Of course, he emailed a rebuttal, but I had already blocked him immediately after I hit the send button.

In response to an email before his last aggressive one to me, I had informed him I would no longer communicate with him. He didn't take it lightly, and that is why he put his disdain of me and our entire office in an email to Liesa, which she neglected to remove from the email thread. When I read the entire email thread and after I made my emoted reply, I was inclined to share it with The Ringmaster as confirmation of my and Danille's statements about Marx' behavior and mistreatment from him and Liesa to the rest of us. Once I showed The Ringmaster the email, he scheduled a meeting in his office with Liesa to ask her about it. She immediately said it did not occur but soon backpedaled after he gave her the email print out. I was so proud of The Ringmaster for having enough gumption, this time, to tell Liesa we would cease communication with Marx and only deal with her, as she was the hired employee.

She tried to change his mind saying she couldn't do all the work; however, The Ringmaster said he wasn't going to allow a stranger to disrespect his staff. Marx had used profanity, cursing me in an email and making sarcastic remarks because of some grammatical corrections I had sent him. Marx even made some chauvinistic remarks regarding me being a woman, which The Ringmaster shared with Liesa. The Ringmaster stood firmly that he wouldn't allow the disrespect of women, as the entire staff was majority women, nor the racially charged statement Marx made and that he fully supported my decision when I told Marx that I would no longer accept his emails or phone calls because of his aggressive behavior and inappropriate emails. Liesa was livid and our relationship was never the same. I said "hi" to her and she responded as if I had asked for her last cigarette.

Liesa would stoop to all levels of low, spouting petty rebuttals and giving trivial excuses and rallying with unhappy interns to engage in the sophomoric behavior she was displaying when it came to completing her tasks and communicating with other staff. It became exhausting to deal with her on a regular basis. It got to the point I resented seeing her, sighing each time she entered the room.

As her supervisor, I had to deal with her the most. No one envied me, especially when I had my weekly communications team meetings, of which she was a key player. It was her, the 90's secretary, and myself, who met under the advice of The Ringmaster, to keep track of what she was doing. She had gone renegade at this point and The Ringmaster was regretting his decision to make her a full-time employee as she had over-promised and under-delivered. It was clear, she wasn't as skilled as she had led on and she would not produce any completed work but would maintain she couldn't attend meetings because she was busy. The work she did complete was weeks late, incorrect, and a poor imitation of past completed work.

I requested her to complete a timeline that I let her set because she would never meet the ones I would set. I assigned her work and let her select a draft deadline and a completion deadline. This didn't work either as she would set a timeline that would allow the team one day to review, which wasn't enough turnaround time and even when we did get it to her, she still wouldn't meet the draft nor the completion deadline.

Liesa simply thought she could do whatever she wanted and whenever she wanted and began to demand people to work around her schedule. She kept extending the deadlines after they passed and documents remained in limbo never seeing a completion date. She was busy trying to become...I actually don't know what she was trying to become but it wasn't what she was hired to do. The situation was all weird and the sad part was that I was her supervisor so I had to deal with all this. This was the mess The Ringmaster had started and left for me to clean up. A monster he had created and then left for me to tame, which I failed to do.

Liesa continued with her antics, losing believers with every excuse and unmet deadline. She had painted a terrible picture to others about our office yet others were witnessing her nonperformance. The fellow staff whose bandwagon she had joined to hate our office, started to disassociate themselves from her. Liesa had so much animosity towards me during the meetings that it felt like every time I said something, I got punched. Every answer was sarcastic and fueled with anger, all unnecessary and irrelevant to the goal of completing the public relations tasks. Things were so bad, the secretary on the communications team insisted I reprimand her for wasting our time and not completing her work.

Our office received continued complaints about the communications work she had not completed. I'm thankful the secretary was a witness and expressed to others that it was Liesa and not our office nor me who didn't process their requests. This set the record straight that it was not my office picking on Liesa but indeed a case of Liesa not fulfilling her tasks because she allowed her anger to get in the way.

The Famine

Liesa's anger and antics became destructive, similar to the devastation of land plagued by locusts. It was a boomerang effect because the deprivation she imposed upon us soon became self-inflicted wounds. There was a specific instance where her defensiveness became a barrier to her completing a simple task. Still doting on her mantra of "I'm so busy, I don't have time to complete anything," Liesa spent an enormous amount of time emailing me instructions on how to complete a task as a prerequisite to her writing an article.

What happened was a manager had requested Liesa to write an article for our website as part of an agreement with a donation he secured. She began emailing me to get information so she could conduct an interview with the donor. No one had asked her to do an interview but just to write a story on the information the manager had presented. I responded, informing her to work with the manager on the content as this was his project. Instead she continued with several emails telling me to conduct research on the donor and send it to her so she could write the article. The manager even reiterated that he wanted to meet with Liesa to go over the information to write the article, yet instead of meeting with him to get the information, she continued to send me emails to get information to her to complete the article.

It was this type of behavior she kept promoting in lieu of performing her job. For some reason, she wanted to engage me in a power struggle when clearly I was the supervisor and she was the subordinate. This is the kind of witnessed behavior that causes people to resign due to the abusive nature. There were other times when I experienced this behavior with her and as a result, it just added to the pile of documentation to support my claim of insubordination and nonperformance. It almost seemed as if I was dealing with Medusa and Bobbi all over again.

The situation with her got out of control to the point she alerted me and the secretary that our communication team meetings were taking up too much of her time, so she would no longer attend until she was caught up on her responsibilities. Then a month later, she sends an email stating she would like to resume the meetings. At that time, I was exhausted and no longer had a tolerance for her behavior. I explained to her the meetings did not stop because she chose not to attend and that we all had responsibilities that we needed to complete; however, we were able to manage our workload while attending the meetings and the additional work we absorbed from her inability to meet deadlines and complete tasks.

Her antics did not stop there. I was informed she had created a website without my knowledge or permission using our donors and corporate partners' names and she had even sent unauthorized emails on behalf of The Ringmaster without his knowledge. Our office found out Liesa was trying to desperately extend her stay, so she would find other projects to do to back up her "I'm so busy" claim, such as trying to facilitate training classes and sit in on meetings she wasn't invited to attend. As darkness turns to light, we also found out she had no academic degree as she had originally indicated, which was a requirement for her position and a general requirement as a trainer. I felt as if The Ringmaster was to blame for this because he allowed her to be a facilitator though she could not provide her college transcripts despite our several requests over a period of months. The reality was, we had been gamed yet again by another con artist.

The Lesson

Liesa taught me a valuable, self-reflective lesson; I was a lousy manager. My hatred toward conflict and laissez faire attitude had me too far in the ocean to ask for a life vest. At that time, I did not understand the profession of management as many great employees are promoted to managers but not properly trained to understand insubordination and how to prevent it. I was not mature enough to handle the structure of managing people. I was a professional at monitoring workloads, completing tasks, meeting deadlines, problem solving, and maintaining the motivation levels of motivated staff. I was a great team member, leader, and follower of instructions, many things I have always been good at, even as a child. All these characteristics, skills, and work ethic got me to a management position but I just did not fully know how to make the transition from employee to manager. In retrospect, I was afraid of the authority and the responsibility authority brings, that I sacrificed my professionalism as my defeat to fear.

For this reason, I am an advocate of management training for organizations. Many companies identify stellar employees and automatically assume their leadership on the job equates to the leadership of being a manager of a group of people. That is not always the case. To be an effective manager requires a different skill set than being an effective employee. Organizations who make these promotions without a plan of action to develop the employee for a management role, are doing that employee, their subordinates, and the entire organization a disservice. Furthermore, those thrusted into management roles must take accountability to seek out management training for themselves.

The Circus had no such training, in fact there was no professional development training offered at all. Professional development was acquired outside of the big top through the traveling facilitators who sent pamphlets months in advance to announce their commercialized workshops at a cost that exceeded most departmental budgets.

If I had some management training, I think I could have deciphered how to establish expectations of my staff and discuss roles in the context of being a leader. However, by the time I decided to "boss up", it was too late. Liesa was out of control because of my fear, my insecurities, my apathy, and my short-comings. I was comfortable taking orders from The Ringmaster and blaming him for things when they went wrong, that I failed my team.

I thought he handled the hiring of Liesa wrong because it was the root that influenced her behavior. Though I felt this way, I should have had a conversation with him to express my concerns because that could have led to setting the expectations and way of work, which Liesa could have chosen to accept or deny the terms. Instead, by complaining in silence, I left it up to Liesa to determine her own standards of operation, which was the opposite of what both The Ringmaster and I had intended.

I also learned the significance of addressing behaviors, good or bad, as they occur to set the standard of what is accepted and what is not. As a manager, you want to reward good/acceptable behaviors and curb bad/unacceptable behaviors so your team understands your expectations for their job performance. I functioned in my management role the same as my personal life, which was to endure unacceptable behavior until I was fed up enough to react. Allowing things to fester without addressing the issue head on leads to resentment, stress, and is simply unfair. Whether it is work or relationships, you must teach people how to treat you. Make your expectations and the consequences for not meeting the expectations clear. If someone chooses not to accept the expectations, then at least they understand what their actions have caused, opposed to not saying anything but holding them accountable to an invisible standard.

As problems persisted, I should have scheduled a meeting with Liesa and The Ringmaster to discuss the challenges and to frankly say, these are the issues and how can we proceed to fix them for the good of the department. I actually remember Liesa trying to repair our working relationship by inviting me to lunch away from the office to settle our problems.

Honestly, I did not want to go because at that time, there was nothing that could change my experience of her nor could it heal the wounds she had inflicted upon me. However, Danille made me realize that though we could not get back to what we had, maybe this meeting could be a start to understand each other and move to a cordial interaction. I had to be open to her gesture because it was an attempt to communicate, which is something I should have initiated months prior. Also, somewhere deep in my heart, I thought this could be the apology I had been waiting for, especially after the disrespectful engagement from her husband.

Unfortunately, after arriving early at the restaurant, she showed up two minutes shy of the 15 minute rule. She ordered her food and we sat down at the table. We were able to discuss that we both had missed the relationship we first had when she arrived. In discussing where it went wrong, she sang her chart topping hit of "I'm so busy" and followed it up with her version of "Me Against the World" that I realized she had no intention of making peace but to approach me as a victim to receive some type of sympathy relief from her assigned work in which I had finally allocated consequences for nonperformance. She had received notice that performance appraisals were approaching and was aware of the significance it would have on her maintaining her position; thus, the purpose of the lunch meeting. Liesa and I agreed to be cordial as neither of us was willing to budge. The damage was done, she made it clear she wasn't going to change her behavior and I was not going to accept her behavior, so I said my good-bye and returned to the office after our 30 minute discussion.

The performance appraisal process with her was intensive. Initially she would not respond to the appraisal review, where her and I would sit down and go over the appraisal. She kept insisting I deliver the appraisal to her office and leave it there. I had to explain to her that the process is a face-to-face meeting, she eventually obliged. However, it was uncomfortable from the time she took a seat in my office.

She had her copy of the appraisal and I had mine. As I went through section by section, Liesa thought she should have all "outstanding" points on her appraisal, though I had actually rated her higher than I truly felt she deserved. The Ringmaster told me to give her a rating of "exceeds expectations" in order to cover up his mishandling of her position. It did not work as Liesa was displeased and refused to sign the appraisal. She was upset

I had rated her "meets expectations" on the Quantity of Work section, which reflected on the prioritizing of work. I had dated examples, thanks to my notes and the communications meetings, to back up the rating. For the Skills and Knowledge section, I gave her an "exceeds expectations" because she over extends herself. Sense of Responsibilities and Cooperation, she received "meets expectations" and I explained to her it was because she refused to do the preliminary work assigned and scheduled other meetings during the time of our standing communications meetings.

Needless to say, Liesa was livid about each rating because it was not "outstanding". She accused me of lying and not understanding the body of work she had completed. Here is another example of the importance of documentation in dealing with folks in toxic environments. I was happy to provide dates of when she did and did not complete tasks via notes and emails. I documented when she gave no notice she wasn't attending meetings and provided documentation of meetings she had with The Ringmaster when she was counseled by him to rectify her rogue behavior.

When I ran down the examples to back up each of my ratings, including instances where she admitted she didn't complete something, she had nowhere to go but to be argumentative. Having documentation disarmed any false accusations and lies she was prepared to use in her defense. During the time I was reviewing the appraisal with her, she seemed uninterested and argued everything I said, even if I repeated something she said. As she provided excuse after excuse in refute to each item from the appraisal, I would respond with an explanation of the documentation and a summary of the conversation. All she could do was give me an attitude, which she gave me a day's worth in a matter of 20 minutes, but I remained calm and stuck to the facts.

I thought I handled it brilliantly. I wanted to argue back but what would it prove? She wanted to get a rise out of me as she spewed insult after insult and at times hitting below the belt. However, I stood my ground on the truth and I knew I was more than fair, so there was no need to engage in nothingness. I was finally being the manager I should have been all along: firm, professional, and by the book. I had the confidence this time because I had the proof, emails, and personal notes attached as backup to everything I stated in the appraisal.

When you stick to the facts, you have a solid foundation to stand on. I went through the entire appraisal, pausing to listen to her rants and then I would say "ok" and move on. She was steaming because she couldn't rattle me and she knew I had proof from all those emails she sent. After exactly 31 minutes, I asked if she had anything else to say, then I gave her the appraisal to sign, which she refused. I didn't press her, I just informed her that I would make a note she was refusing to sign and would submit it with the others. I thanked her for her time and she stormed out.

When you are put in situations where other parties are expressing their anger, remain calm and unbothered as not to match negativity with negativity. Just as darkness is overcome with light and hate with love, so is negativity with positivity. Your goal should not be to succumb to the toxicity in the workplace but to overcome it by realizing you are above it. When you rise above the toxicity, you have control and the upper hand. Actually, this hurts them more than going back and forth with them. I held onto my peace and I just saw her as pathetic as she left angrily. I felt great and relieved knowing I had finally done the right thing, the right way and most importantly, with my documentation, it was not an emotional move but it was professional, strictly based on the best for the organization and the morale of the department.

I thank Liesa for teaching me a hard lesson in not addressing the problem right when it happens. I, like so many others, when something goes wrong or is not right, ignore it the first couple of times and in management, that will only come to bite you in the rear. You must address the problem when it happens and say why it's wrong and demonstrate how it should be or state your expectations along with letting them know the repercussions if the behavior continues. There is no reason to write someone up on the first offense (this depends on the magnitude), compassion is part of management, but you need to address it along with an understanding of why it happened. Follow up with a consequence, so they know the outcome in case they choose to make the same mistake. This will prevent hearing the statement 'well I've been doing this for awhile and you never said anything before'. No, say something and then make sure you document it in your records, so if things take a turn for the worse, you actually have proof, written documentation and not a battle of hearsay of their word against yours.

Toxic environments attract and produce toxic people. Liesa distributed typical toxic behavior: going rogue, defying the rules, refusing to communicate, blaming others for their actions, sabotaging work, not working to the goal of the organization, and contributing to an unhealthy work environment. Lying was the foundation of her toxicity, which we know has its roots in threat management response.

Remaining sure of yourself, documenting, keeping calm, being proactive and not reactive, and sticking to the facts is how you can overcome situations like that of Liesa. I learned to take control and to take authority as a manager. I must admit, she did a number on our department but we were all relieved when budget cuts came around and The Ringmaster chose to save a couple of positions by laying Liesa off. The irony was because of the lay off, she could not come back, even as a consultant, for at least a year. I remember looking out the window as an intern helped her take her belongings to her car. It was a long battle but finally, I could exhale.

8   COLD AS ICE MEANS BE TWICE AS NICE

'Art imitates life' and 'life imitates art' creates a debate among creatives, like the proponents of the chicken and egg, in determining which came first. As Oscar Wilde challenged the Aristotelians in this paradox, the importance of the order pales to the correlation of art and life. The two go together in expressing perceptions and realities in a metaphoric disposition to communicate a feeling beyond words. Music is an art that brings a resonance to how we feel or what we have experienced.

My life, like many of yours, in its ups and downs can be described through a musical score of various artists over the decades, like a soundtrack to a blockbuster movie. The heartbreak anthems of Brandy, Boyz II Men, Mary J. Blige, and the Waiting to Exhale soundtrack helped me through the conclusions of pivotal romantic relationships. Whereas "One More Chance", "This is How We Do It", "My Boo", "Let Me Clear My Throat", "Don't Stop Til You Get Enough" and "Lights, Camera, Action" send me down memory lane on dance floors around the world. It's the genres of Motown, Disco, Gospel, R&B, Hip Hop, Rock, and Pop that have shared in chronicling my life's chapters. Regardless of the experience, my memories are tied to music.

In my work settings, music has always played in the backdrop; primarily, providing comfort and noise as I write, work on projects, and fulfill a day's work. At times, music has been a descriptive in my dealings with personalities on the job. Two songs come to mind when I think about Miss Payne, a manager at The Circus. Foreigners' "Cold as Ice" and Dr. Suess' "The Grinch" would provide tell-all lyrics and sentiments to describe the toxicity which traveled through the veins and spewed from the lips of Miss Payne aka the Ice Queen, of whom is the subject of this chapter.

"You're cold as ice...you never take advice, someday you'll pay the price" paired with "You're a mean one, Mr. Grinch; your heart's an empty hole; you're as cuddly as a cactus, you're as charming as an eel" can best describe the attitude of Miss Payne. She stood about 5 '6, late 40's, slender but not thin, adorning a daily frown from the moment she arrived into the parking lot until her car drove down the street.

Everyday you could find Miss Payne interview ready, dressed in a dark skirt suit, falling just below her knees with the matching blazer and some type of neutral colored shirt and black low heeled pumps and flesh-toned hosiery. At times, she'd switch up and throw on some loose fitting, straight-leg pants with a heavy short cardigan, if she didn't whip out the ole pantsuit. She wore her hair, straight, at the middle of her neck and her bangs were swooped to the side. I think out of the eight years we worked in the same building, she changed her hair once, getting a trendy short cut which looked nice. Miss Payne always upheld a conservative appearance, branding herself as the resident human resource manager.

The irony about Miss Payne was she fit into a niche category of human resource professionals who were not people-oriented. How can you be in the position to help employees acclimate to jobs with a foul-attitude and discriminatory practices? It was something the entire staff discreetly discussed as pointed out by interns, visitors, and community partners who had felt the cool breeze from the Ice Queen.

The Ice Queen took her throne in a suite which included a huge office and space to conduct interviews and set-up her annual simulations. Typically she received an intern who had to have special skills, per her request, which was totally understandable to work in that office. Her request was the worker be mature with a professional attitude to make calls to organizations and individuals and to assist with interview preparation. Most importantly, the intern had to have the type of personality worthy of pleasing the Ice Queen.

Out of all her interns, which none lasted over a year, I never had an issue with any of them. My job required interaction with her office and over the years I found her workers to be personable, hardworking, and reliable. However, it was one intern who seemed quiet but soon took on the personality of her owner, I mean boss. In doing so, she began to violate policies and display disrespectful behavior to the staff in my office, in the same manner as the Ice Queen. She'd soon find out who actually was the boss.

You're a Mean One

The Ice Queen and I had general menial differences in our ways of work; however, none of them posed a problem except for one, our treatment of people. I am and always have been an advocate for the underdog and it itches me to the core when I see someone getting the short end of the stick for no apparent reason.

This stems from my childhood. In elementary, I was befriended by Brandy W., who seemed like she was 5'8 in the third grade. When we lined up, by height, for the bathroom break, she was always at the back of line with the boys. In addition to her height and size, she took on bullying girls as a defense mechanism from the bullying of the boys in our class. I would stand up for her, not because I liked her but because I thought it was wrong in how she was being treated.

This caused me to be invited to all of her birthday parties throughout elementary. I must admit Brandy's mom gave her some great parties. There was always plenty of good food, like pizza and burgers, a themed birthday cake, games, and the best goodie bags. Brandy was an only child, so her mom typically went all out for her and was very nice; however, her daughter did not share the same gracious hospitality. The fact was, despite her parties being great, I nor anyone else wanted to attend because Brandy would bully us at her own party. I was always baffled as to how someone would invite people to their party and then verbally insult them and push them. Brandy's mom would step in and tell her to stop. I remember once, her mom said "Brandy if you keep doing that, you won't have any friends". The truth was she already did not have any friends, we were coming because of the food, games, and gifts. However, Brandy's bullying had gotten so bad that certain classmates would throw her invitation in the trash as not to show their parents, so they wouldn't have to attend. If the other kids went to her party, it was only because I was going and they would tell their parents to pick them up before or at the same time my mom had planned to get me.

Dealing with Brandy W. was a foretaste of my taking abuse at the hand of the one I was defending. By the time the Ice Queen rolled into my life, this would be second nature to me. For some reason, standing up for an underdog has always found a way to bite me in the rear. I have so many stories of how Brandy became my worst female enemy in elementary simply because she took my kindness for friendship. Being friends has to be mutually beneficial but being kind to people is sometimes a one way standard because it is a personality characteristic.

A trait the Ice Queen did not possess was kindness. She hand-picked interns to prepare for corporate interview sessions instead of offering the opportunity to all company interns seeking full-time employment. During this time, The Circus had open recruitment, meaning anyone who graduated from high school or earned a GED or was enrolled at a university regardless of grade point average, could intern at The Circus. With this type of recruitment strategy, naturally some applicants were rough around the edges, but if our organization was built on providing equal opportunity for employment, then so should be the treatment of all applicants turned interns. With an open recruitment strategy, the expectation of additional patience and care may be needed when helping interns but choosing not to help them develop for job opportunities with The Circus was reinforcing the oppressive environments these interns were trying to escape.

The Ice Queen's approach to interns and temporary employees earned the disdain many had for her. Interns and temps continuously complained of the lack of training and development offered to help them get onboarded and prepare for full time employment, which was their reasoning for applying for the program. Many went as far as complaining to The Ringmaster. In addition to her preferential treatment of certain interns, the Ice Queen's know-it-all attitude and refusal to build relationships outside of three corporate partners, irritated me.

I was not alone in my sentiments toward the Ice Queen; however, there were a few needles in a haystack who thought the world of Miss Payne. One of the interns is one of my good friends who had a positive experience with her, in fact they remain in contact until this day. He describes her as extremely supportive as an intern turned professional. She came to his masters graduation and even to his father's funeral nine years after The Circus. There are other former interns she supported and I think that is tremendous, but as I explained to him, he was one of the chosen few.

If you were an exceptional intern who only needed a little polishing, she would extend her services. The average intern or temp with less experience coupled with an urban appearance had to change their appearance to get the career development services from her office. There was no muddy waters with the Ice Queen, you were either in or out and the majority of interns and staff were out, especially if you worked in The Ringmaster's office.

I remember her nearly disowning her former intern when that worker decided to work for my office instead of hers. In fairness, The Ringmaster did approach the intern and offer her more pay (he basically stole the intern), so the Ice Queen was naturally angry with him. However, I felt she was out of line to take that anger out on the worker. Money talks and for a starving college student, money shouts. Blame should not have been placed on the intern but Miss Payne did and that was cold!

You Never Take Advice

Though our ways of treating people were juxtaposed, I initially didn't have a problem with the Ice Queen. For several years we co-existed and kept a cordial relationship with occasional interaction of our crossing yet never intersecting paths. The tribulation came when I received a promotion which consisted of managing the overall staff performance measures and reorganization of the staff positions in the department.

She expressed to The Ringmaster her concern with my being so young, not being mature enough to handle confidentiality and being too inexperienced to effectively complete the job. My promotion was not a supervisory role over her position or operation but over operational systems, which included roles in various organizational committees. This was yet another management opportunity I thought would solidify my desire to finally "make it"; however, it would result in being another mountain I'd have to climb.

Medusa had always complained about working with Ice Queen because she refused to follow the established branding guidelines for promotional materials and was overall difficult to work with because of her attitude, which she described as "sour". While Medusa was in office, I never had to experience the infamous tude. However, getting this promotion caused Medusa to become excited, when she would normally complain any other time I received a promotion or an accolade. Essentially, I was taking a problem off her hands and freeing her time to conjure ways to torture me later on in the year.

My mistake with Ice Queen was yielding to her prejudice of younger women having authority, which clearly was embedded in the company's culture, because this was not my first nor last time going down this road. I failed to realize that though she had those feelings towards me, it was irrelevant to my ability to perform my job; it was her issue to bear, not mine. As a new manager, it was another hard lesson where I lost the battle before suiting up. How could I expect her to respect me in this position when I had already consented to being disrespected.

With the promotion, I became in charge of the content for the department's internal correspondence and communications, including: a newsletter, announcements, and videos on the company's television monitors. Procedures were in place for anyone wanting something displayed to submit to me so that I could ensure it coincided with our branding, was grammatically correct, and tasteful. This was something Medusa had previously coordinated which was now my responsibility.

It would turn out to be a thorn in my side, particularly because Ice Queen was demanding and refused to follow the guidelines when submitting information for these media outlets. She would always give me items to approve the day she wanted it placed on the monitor. I would share with her each time the procedures and each time she got irritated that I was reinforcing the guidelines; often telling me she did not have time to submit the information to me in advance and that she felt it should not take too much of my time to approve her items for posting.

I was appalled by her total inconsideration of my time, as if I had nothing else to do but wait on her random mistake laden submissions. Then when I would send her the content revisions, she always had a rebuttal that I was being "too harsh" and that my revisions were "irrelevant and minor". These comments came from someone who refused to help certain interns get job opportunities because they did not meet her standards, but yet wanted flyers with misspelled words and slang-ridden phrases to appear on tv monitors to advertise her events. I could not believe the hypocrisy!

I continued to approve her items on last minute notice coupled with an explanation of the guidelines, thinking she would be mature and stop. However, she never stopped because she simply had no intentions to do so, she never had when Medusa was handling this task and definitely not for me, a person she clearly did not respect. Her actions in this manner became so frequent, that I finally had to break down and follow my own guidelines that I preached to her and disapprove of one of her last minute items due to untimely submission.

She was highly upset and argued with me that I should approve the document on the grounds I had done it before. She was right, I continued to bend the rules for her because I was afraid of the conflict but this avoidance made things worse. I reached a point where I was fed up with her attitude and overall disrespect. I reminded her just like she doesn't have time to get things to me in advance, I don't have time to look at her last minute work. I also shared the concept that if the items were as important as she indicated they were, she would have worked on them ahead of time to ensure the timely display of the announcements.

The Ringmaster would later back me in this statement as my supervisor had previously warned me that my leniency would soon come back to bite me. And it sure did, it was Brandy W. all over again. My kindness to Brandy also bit me during the annual field day games when she signed up on every team I was on in order to throw the race to ensure I wouldn't win. She had done this because I had refused to call her when she asked me to. As a result, I was the only student in my class to not win ribbons during the annual field day and I was one of the most athletic kids in my grade and was on winning teams. It was so bad my teacher went and bought me a yellow participation ribbon as consolation for her not believing me and my friends when we told her what Brandy was planning as we were signing up for field day teams. I pleaded with the teacher and my friends asked her to remove Brandy from my teams but she did not and just said we were being ridiculous. I was beyond devastated because I always have been a true competitor; I'd rather have nothing than to have a participation ribbon. At least with nothing, I could claim I was never there but the ribbon signifies that not only was I there but I came up empty handed, five times! Who wants to culminate that?!

I regret that it took me so long to realize my kindness was leading me into passiveness and I needed to learn the difference because I was failing. It was the small kind gestures like the previously described that would only become the foundation of a blowout between Ice Queen and myself but would define our relationship forever. It was the turning point to realize there was no turning back to cultivate a cordial relationship, especially on her part. She was through with me and if I thought she treated me badly before, I was wrong. After not approving her document, our interaction had worsened to the point of hatred. If I was her, I would have hated me too because I got the best of her at a time when she yielded to her emotions.

You're a Foul One

The Ice Queen had an intern who was no doubt a hard worker (Lyla) but just because someone is a hard worker, doesn't give you the right to make them work full time hours when they are part-time. The nitty gritty was that interns were not staff members. Staff members applied to a public job posting and went through a series of interviews and a hiring process conducted by human resources to be hired as a full-time employee. Interns were full-time university students or recent high school graduates who held jobs within departments at The Circus as a way to gain experience. There was a limit to the amount of hours they could work because their primary focus was being a student. These jobs consisted of odds and end tasks to work anywhere from 10-30 hours a week. Thirty hours was rare and was mostly given to graduate students, where 20 hours was the norm for undergraduate students.

The intern distinction and process was not the first rodeo for Ice Queen as she had several interns in the past, which all operated under the standard 20 hour a week limit, for all undergraduates. During this time, I was the supervisor to the accounts payable clerk, Danille, who oversaw payroll and supervised intern hours and pay for our department. Danille had informed me she had received a timesheet from Lyla who recorded a 30 hour surplus for the entire month. Interns were paid monthly, so they would turn in their timesheets which designated the hours worked weekly for the month. Because Miss Payne is the Ice Queen, Danille informed me she didn't want to speak to her about it as she has had a previous issue with Lyla violating the 20 hour limit and she had corrected it. However, this time was overboard. So as a manager, it is my job to step in and provide a resolution.

I sent an email to Ice Queen informing her of the 20 hour work week rule and noted Lyla's 30 hour overage as a policy violation which would need to be adjusted to incorporate the 30 hours that had already been worked. Meaning, the 30 hours can't be applied to the month she worked but will be applied the next month, so basically, only allow her to work 50 hours instead of 80 hours. Letting her intern violate the hour policy was not anyone else's fault because it is the responsibility of the intern's supervisor to keep track of their worker's hours and in doing so, to approve, by signature, the timesheet before submission to Danille. However, that is not the way Ice Queen perceived it.

Instead of following the guidelines and being happy the guidelines were being enforced, this time, Ice Queen sent me emails telling me who I needed to speak with regarding her interpretation of the rules. She felt her intern should get paid more than the others and demanded a reclassification of Lyla in order for this to happen. In the meantime, Lyla had already acknowledged she should not have worked the hours because she was aware of the 20 hour limit and was fine with the arrangement of having to work less the next month because of her overage.

Danille and I had even worked it out to give Lyla some extra money to make up for the inconvenience she suffered on behalf of her supervisor who actually requested Lyla to work more hours, despite knowing the rules. Danille ensured Lyla understood if she worked over again, regardless, she would have to report this direct violation.

From this point, the cables of communication got tangled between Ice Queen and Lyla because Ice Queen claimed Lyla never took part in the conversation Danille and I had with her about the violation and the extra funds. Ice Queen went as far as to tell Danille and I, in an email, how we should pay Lyla and to add insult to injury, she copied Lyla on the email. At that point, I had enough of Ice Queen and her hypocrisy, condescending attitude, discriminatory practices, and sophomoric antics. My background with her reared its ugly head in my mind and so I decided to give her a piece of it.

Ice Queen spoke to The Ringmaster about the situation and when he upheld the 20 hour a week policy, she stormed out of his office. Therefore, he sent her an email stating since she couldn't talk to him and felt the need to walk out on their meeting, he would no longer be involved with this issue, restated that I was in charge and any further issues regarding interns, she would have to consult myself, Geppetto, or Danille.

The Ringmaster's support and email made her even more angry. She came to my office to have some choice words with me, in which I tried to explain the policy that I had already explained several times before; however, she just walked away after giving me the attitude about how I was going to pay Lyla regardless and the policy didn't apply to her.

I should have left the issue there as it had already been resolved. Danille and I had already explained everything more than twice to her and we had proof that Lyla understood our resolve with the hours and pay. The Ice Queen was the one who kept trying to change the rules and I should have left her alone to deal with what she refused to accept. However, I kept trying to explain as if it really was going to make a difference. Me and my hard lessons.

The demands for Lyla to get paid kept coming and I kept responding, with the situation hitting a peak via email I sent to Miss Payne hoping to resolve everything. I started the email off with *Note: I encourage you to save this email, read it in its entirety, and use it as a point of reference as I will clearly answer all questions associated with this matter, as this will be my final comment on this particular situation.* And this is where I stooped to her level. I had literally reached my breaking point. In sending the long email, I made sure I copied her lying intern, Lyla, since she continued to have amnesia about our numerous conversations. I copied Danille as she had numerous conversations with both of the repeat offenders.

I spelled everything out in the email. I wrote *Concern 1: Intern Hours*, then I labeled *Answer:* and stated the policy. The second concern was Lyla's hourly rate, third was her back pay, fourth was her being classified as "something else" and the fifth was the coverage of the front desk in Ice Queen's office, which she complained she needed. I stuck to the facts in my answers by repeating the policies. I was certain this email would be the end all because I had a few people read it before I sent it and they said it was to the point but well needed for who and what type of behavior I was dealing with.

In hindsight, I was wrong in copying Lyla. I copied her on the email out of retaliation from a prior demeaning email Ice Queen had sent me, where she copied Lyla, causing her to become disrespectful to my office staff when Lyla had been pleasant before Payne's email. That email and Lyla's behavior, coupled with the fact she (Lyla) had lied, awakened the vengeful scorpio in me and it became my intention to set the record straight and sting the both of them. That's why it is important to rethink things before doing them, seek counsel before having difficult conversations verbally or through email. It was like all the years of me allowing Miss Payne to suppress me rose up and said *"We're not going to take it" and so you want to play with fire, so today's your day to get burned*...and that is what happened. She never responded to the email and when I let someone read the email in its entirety, they said "How could she? There is nothing for her to say...you laid it all out." Boy, did I feel good. I finally stuck it to her and in writing where she could read it over and over.

I guess it bothered her so much, she didn't enter our office for another month. In fact, she didn't even send another email for almost two months. It worked! I had finally gotten through to her and this issue had been put to rest...or so I thought. During the time out from her, the office had commended me for preventing her negativity from invading our office. I still today do not know what was going on in her head those two months of hiatus but she had not let it go.

She broke her silence by forwarding my email to The Ringmaster and blind copying me. He questioned why he was being sent an email from over two months ago on an issue that had been resolved. I told him "I don't know, maybe she wanted you to read it."

I too was a little shocked she would resurface the email after a lapse of time. Did it take her two months to decide to check an email from me? Did it take her two months to cool off? Was she thinking of a master plan to hurt me or not physically hurt me? I don't know but after an idle two months, you would think a person would just move on. I could have said worse things, so I was surprised she had taken it so hard, given the way she treated people on a regular basis. Who knew Ice Queen had feelings? Furthermore, apparently she not only had feelings but was extremely sensitive to letting a little email fester.

During the two months, The Ringmaster mentioned she had not been communicating with him as well. He had reached out to her to conduct some mock interviews with interns and attend a board meeting, in which she was to send some information to me. What did he do? He put me in the ring with the pit bull and told me to send her an email. I secretly thought he liked the fact that we didn't get along and that I was finally hated by someone, because normally people loved me and spoke highly of me, thanks to God's favor.

Well, she responded to my email and copied The Ringmaster and stated she was not going to do the report for the board meeting because the two day request was short notice. However, she did not respond about the mock interviews, which were a separate issue that had no connection with the board meeting. I replied to her email, with The Ringmaster copied, and asked about whether or not she was going to conduct the interviews. What did I do that for? She responded to me only with "This is the last time you will address me in an email with your attitude. If you would read what I wrote...obviously not!" Ahh, and there it was, she's still angry.

I didn't think I had an attitude when I sent her the email "Mock interviews...Will you be able to conduct them? If so, what time?" Maybe it was the three periods that sent her over the edge again. It was evident she had intentionally not responded to the mock interview questions because she was still mad and perturbed that no one cared. Her animosity towards me had gotten the best of her, altering how she performed in her role. She sent the attitude email prematurely and it made her look bad because The Ringmaster then asked me, "What is wrong with her? Why would she send that email to you? Has something happened between the two of you?"

I proceeded to inform The Ringmaster of the many years of interaction with Ice Queen and how it had changed from being cordial to turmoil with every promotion I received. I told him examples of how she had spoken down to me through email and in person and her having the attitude towards me was nothing new. The difference was I finally stood up for myself and didn't allow her to suppress me and she did not like it. He said, "Oh so that's why she hasn't been in the office. I thought she was mad at me because I mentioned her walking out on our meeting." He said that he was going to speak to her and have a meeting with the both of us to settle the score.

Before he could do that, there was a general meeting scheduled in which the three of us were in, plus about five others. The entire time she wouldn't even make eye contact with me or The Ringmaster. You could feel the animosity and the bad aura about her; she was pissed, to say the least. It was almost scary because you never know what someone is going through and this might have been the last straw before she went postal! On the inside I felt like something was going to happen. She was not letting it go, I just knew she was going to say something sarcastic. Moreover, I believed she was waiting for me to say anything, so she could unload her built up anger on me.

However, The Ringmaster made it a quick meeting, as not to let anyone speak about anything unless they were called upon. That was a change in pace because normally his meetings are long and pointless as to let everyone say whatever they want. Once he concluded the meeting, she said sternly, "I need to meet with both of you now." The Ringmaster responds "Ok, you both can come to my office." I take a deep breath and Danille looks at me like "good luck" with big eyes and slight head tilt like I don't know what's about to happen but it can't be good.

I walked into his office last, with the email proof in my hand and sat in the left chair facing his desk as she sat in the right chair facing him, which is next to my chair but separated by three feet. The Ringmaster takes his place behind the big cherrywood desk facing us, sitting upright with his hands folded. She is sitting straight up as well with her legs crossed at the ankles under the chair. I'm nervous sitting at the edge of my chair because I got receipts in the emails to prove it is her who indeed has the attitude and it's me just trying to enforce policies.

The Ringmaster then opens up the dialogue by telling both of us he has read the emails we have sent back and forth to each other and by no means should we have included the interns on any of the emails unless the email was to the actual intern. He then proceeds to go on about how we both are God-fearing women and we go to church on the regular and blah blah blah. At that point, I was like, *you are no one's spiritual counselor, so maybe you need to stick to what you know and leave the soul saving to Jesus the Christ Himself.*

After his sermon, he gives Ice Queen the floor, and she immediately starts shouting at me, close to the top of her lungs, regarding how I should respect her position as a manager. This catches The Ringmaster off guard as when she began, he did a double take with his head, like he thought his church speech had calmed the seas and we would actually have a civilized conversation. How can that be when you don't have two civilized people in the room? As she yells at me, I make no eye contact with her and I lean back in my chair because I know she has just now lost the fight. She proved what I had been saying for years about her attitude towards me. While she's shouting, I look at The Ringmaster, who is wide-eyed in surprise at what he is witnessing, and say very calmly, "See this is how she talks to me all the time."

He then tries to calm her down and say "let's talk about…" but she cuts him off in response to the statement I made during her rant. I was shocked she could yell and listen at the same time..well just really shocked she could listen, because up until that day, I didn't know she had that capability. She yells, even louder "That's right, this is how I talk to you! You don't respect me! I'm your elder!" The truth came out, which I knew all along. She did not like the fact that I was younger than her and occupying the position I had. At that time I was in my mid to late 20's and she was in her late 40's, early 50's. This is just further proof of the importance in understanding the generational dynamics in the workplace.

At this point, I was wondering what to do. I look at The Ringmaster and say "This is what I deal with all the time." As he continues to stare in shock at not only how loud she is but the level of venom in her entire posture and facial expressions. She looked like she was literally about to physically attack someone. If she did, I had already eyed his name plate, as with one lunge toward me, I would act fast to protect myself with it. She literally looked like she was about to bite; she had a ferocious look in her eyes and fangs were out. I hadn't noticed them before until that day. The whole situation happened so quickly, like when Michael Jackson turned around with a wolf head in Thriller during the romantic walk in the park. I was startled, do I run or do I sit there, where do we go from here?

The Ringmaster firmly jumps in with a tone that your parents would use when you are close to getting a punishment if you did not adhere to their last pleas "Listen, you have got to calm down." But Noooo! she comes back with "I don't have to calm down! I'm mad!" That's when I made eye contact with her for the first time in two months, in unbelief in how she was continuing to behave. She had justified her erratic behavior with the reasoning of being mad. I looked her dead in her eye and snickered and then shook my head and faced The Ringmaster. I think it was then she realized she had made an absolute fool of herself.

Finally, the truth revealed itself completely. I felt vindicated and I saw in my mind, as she got up and ran out the office, Muhammad Ali in the boxing ring with his gloves up as the people chanted "Ali, Ali, Ali!" After all these years, she showed in a few minutes, more than I could ever tell of how she treated me. The Ringmaster then apologized and said "What is wrong with her? I see it now." And that was the day I got my power back. I realized I no longer had to walk on eggshells because someone else had a problem with me, my age, or my position. I would always choose to take the high road and be calm so as not to get into an argument with someone just because I felt mistreated. I was there to do my job and I knew I had a future ahead of me because I was talented and anyone who had a problem with my age, well it was exactly that, their problem.

We would not have any more blow ups after that as she pretty much stayed out of my way and when she needed to communicate with me, she sent messages through the office receptionist and things worked out that way.

The only other time she would have a chance to snap on me was one day I was in the front office talking to someone and she said "Where is Juan?" So I kept on talking since she had not spoken with me in years. Then she repeated herself, and stood there staring at me. I said with surprise "Are you asking me?" she says "Yes, who else would I be asking?" I started looking around because there were three other people where I was...*why me? especially when you don't talk to me...remember the last time you were mad and told The Ringmaster you could not communicate with me.* I kept my cool as everyone else was looking to understand what was going on. I replied, "I don't know who Juan is." Then I continued with my conversation she had rudely interrupted, proving nothing had changed except the fact that everybody knew she was rude. The Ringmaster had told everyone in the office how she had behaved herself in our last meeting.

Then she says in a real nasty tone while snaking her head "You know exactly who I'm talking about. That's why I hate talking to you cause you trying to be smart. Juan, Juan, you know the girl that sits at the front." By this time, everyone in the office had stopped their side conversations and were looking at her like why is she so angry and her tone was so unnecessary. I then said "Oh you mean, LaWanna, she's not here." She replies very snippily,

"You knew who I was talking about in the first place, you just trying to be smart."

I then responded, "I thought you said Juan and I honestly didn't know who that was." As she heads towards the door she continues to gripe about how I knew who she was talking about. Then one of the persons in the front, who happened to be a staff member said, "What is wrong with her?" I said, "I don't know, it's Monday." The staff member starts to laugh and says "I was just about to ask you, when did y'all hire a boy named Juan. I was curious too where he was at because LaWanna has worked here for months, so why would she call her Juan?"

Someday You'll Pay the Price

The saying goes, until you smash the head of a snake, it does not die. My grandmother used to tell me about how when she was a child, in order to kill a particular snake, they had to get rid of the head. She said chopping it in half would not kill it because it would mend itself back together if you did not separate the parts far enough from each other. Well after a year, Ice Queen decided to come for me via email by sending me job duties. She sent one telling me to email everyone in the building notifying them there are reserved parking spots in the front because she has "been patience[sic] enough and do not feel that I have to make accommodations for myself when I pay a "hefty" price for reserved parking." She was absolutely right, if you have a reserved spot then you should be able to park in it. However, I'm not the building manager who helped you get your treasured spot, so maybe you should start with the person whose job it is and you should know that because you turned your information and payment into her to order the spot.

When she realized I ignored her parking spot email, a few months later she sent me an email at 4:08pm and everyone got off at 5pm, telling me she needed a recommendation letter written by 12 noon the next day. Here we have another last minute request and then you did not have the courtesy to ask nor send a greeting like "hi" or "I know this is short notice but…". She starts the email off with "I need a recommendation letter….". The Ice Queen reared her toxic head again because after she didn't get the letter at the time she had designated me to do so, she wrote an email to The Ringmaster tattling on me for not getting it done when she said. The funny part was in the tattle email, she notes she didn't speak to me directly about the letter and when she came to get the letter, she found out I wasn't even at work that day. Tell me how much sense does it make to tattle on someone who is out of the office? It's like getting fired on your day off. How can I read your email when I'm not in the office? (we did not have access to our emails offsite, like we do now) Insanity.

One thing to realize in the workplace, especially one that is toxic, some people will just have it in for you. I felt like Ice Queen kept trying to get some type of revenge on me for her ridiculous actions in that office blowout. I gave her absolutely no ammunition. She kept constantly shooting blanks and each time she tried to start something, she would just continue to show how unprofessional and rude she was and it became obvious she had a vendetta against me. It became apparent because the more I ignored her and chose not to respond to her attempts to provoke me, she kept trying harder and it earned her a denotion on her annual performance review, because she had received a warning yet she continued.

The write up was a result of her blaming me for something a faculty member did that she wanted to do and the Ice Queen started again to give me orders via email but this time she copied an intern in one of her ignorant rants. It had gotten to the point that I couldn't even explain something to her without her thinking I was trying to sabotage her. It's funny because I truly understand the saying *it's a thin line between love and hate*. The same energy it takes to love someone is the same in hating someone and she hated me. I was constantly on her mind and no matter what I said she would always seem to think the worst, just as you would when someone you love disappoints you. It becomes hard for you to trust them because you don't want to go down that path of hurt again. It's unfortunate and it's also hilarious that people who hate you for some reason think you hate them and thus are consumed with them. The fact is, that other person probably, as I did, could care less about you and maybe that is what hurts the most. They are unbothered by you and thus are not out to get you because they hold no feelings towards you but your hate and hurt won't see it and therefore, you go around harboring ill feelings toward someone who doesn't even think about you. That energy could be put to something positive and productive.

It was no secret Ice Queen hated me and thought I was out to get her. I had no need. Yet another time, she wanted to be an advisor for an organization that I had, along with a few others, charted after the local professional branch of the organization. She showed up unannounced at one of our meetings and when she walked in she looked at me and said, "I want to be the advisor" and walked off to sit in a seat across the room. No hello, no discussion, no inquiry as to how the advisory role works, nothing. Unbeknownst to her and me too, the members had already asked another staff member to be their primary advisor, as I would remain as the administrative advisor to ensure the success of the official charter.

In short, she sent an email to me angry that I did not make her the advisor and had assigned someone else. I explained to her that the members had asked the staff member to be their advisor and that person then sent an email to The Ringmaster stating her commitment to the organization in that role. I did not find out this was done until The Ringmaster informed me of it. I explained this to her and mentioned I had told the members to add Ice Queen as the staff advisor in my place in the following semester, once the charter had been received.

I went out of my way to give her what she demanded and she still resulted in calling me a liar because it did not happen on her terms. She claimed the members did not choose the staff member but I did even though there was email proof the members chose her, especially because I had no knowledge they had selected anyone. She went on to say "Since you failed to clarify or even mention this when we met last week, I can see where they [sic] confusion lies."

Again, she continues to send emails without proofreading and has the nerve to wonder why I ignore her. You can't discriminate against interns when your grammar is subpar. Then she said she and I had meetings when we don't even communicate. We didn't meet, that requires us scheduling a time and a place with a purpose in mind and second we didn't have a conversation, which requires both of us speaking on a mutual topic. She made a statement and immediately walked off. Lastly, I told the interns they needed to find an advisor and they did and it was not Miss Payne. Her delusions and perception that I was out to get her was further confirmation to me that she suffered from paranoid personality disorder, just like Floral.

The Lesson

The people make the place and toxic people make a toxic environment. Miss Payne, the Ice Queen was a toxic individual, often dishing out what she could not take. She projected her insecurities, anger, and unhappiness onto others. One thing you will find as you work in various environments is that misery loves company and hurt people, hurt people.

My experience with Ice Queen is such an unfortunate common one. There are just instances where you can do all you can, extend the olive branch until it forms a tree and some people will just not like you. The irony is you may think it's something you did or did not do but when you boil it down, it really has nothing to do with you but more of them, so don't ever take their attacks personally, no matter how many times they come for you.

Ice Queen taught me a lot about a major insecurity within myself. I was taught to respect my elders and I think in the workplace you have to know how to draw the line between respect and disrespect. My shyness, age, and upbringing had formed a humbleness that made me uncomfortable in being authoritative. I lacked courage in standing up for myself, thinking I always had to show respect to others. However, I needed to learn that respect did not mean bowing down to others nor allowing someone to be disrespectful to me. I failed to realize my family had given me the tools to be courageous, I just had to believe in myself.

My first mistake with Ice Queen was I did not draw the line of respect. If I had set guidelines for everyone to follow, I should have held her to those without buckling. My not upholding the guidelines with her and not standing firm on what I said, made me weak in her eyes and further confirmed the ageist thoughts of incapability she had towards me. I counted myself out in the beginning by not setting expectations of how I wanted to be treated in that position. She basically had me in a box and as long as I stayed in the box of being a young girl holding a coordinator position, she was fine with me. As soon as I began to get promoted and gain authority, some that she had none over, at my age, then she developed a problem with me. Being young does not disqualify you for any position and just because of your age, it is your knowledge and experience that qualifies you, so assume the authority given to you. Do not abuse your power but do not give it away either. Set expectations on how you want to be treated.

When someone has an issue with you, do go the extra mile to make things right. Keep the line of communication open by pulling that person aside and having a one-on-one to come to an early resolution. If after extending the courtesy and the person still has a disdain towards you, then keep your composure and move on and let them deal with their problem. Do not do what I did and stoop to their level of insults. Do not give them power to get you out of your character nor tarnish your name over silly and unprogressive interactions. If you give them this power, you succumb to everything they are, which is not a positive place to be. You have to learn to take the high road at all times and know you are made for greater things and this situation is just a test. You have to take responsibility for your reactions and choose to be proactive.

Being reactive will cause you to lose every time because you are playing their game, which means you are not on your game. You have to choose to remain calm and not argue with them. Remember, when you argue with a fool, no one can tell the difference. When dealing with them, make it brief and if you have to communicate via email, always have someone you can copy or bcc, so that if you need proof later on, you can pull it up and someone else has a copy. Preferably, you want to cc your supervisor on all communications with that person, so they are aware of the communication thread and can see for themselves what is transpiring so they can step in where necessary. Before copying your supervisor, make sure you have a talk with them about the nature of the relationship you have with this person, so they are aware.

When I look back on all my interactions with Ice Queen, I shake my head and laugh. I must admit, my fondest memory was when she went off in The Ringmaster's office and I did not play into her hand and she ended up looking like a heel. It was then I began to feel sorry for her because it was evident she was an angry woman with deeply rooted issues towards younger women in positions of authority and some unhappiness within herself.

Knowing you have the power to take control of the situation is always key to surviving toxic environments. Of course, documentation is a life-saving tactic and staple in dealing with toxicity. Also, knowing when to just be quiet and walk away, even to the point of ignoring someone, is pivotal when you have a relentless attacker. Remember Erykah Badu's line "What good do your words do if they can't understand you, don't go talking that sh*t." This statement has never been more true in situations where people only see things their way and not through a logical lens. There is nothing you can say to make a person who does not want to understand to understand, so stop talking because at that point, you are getting nowhere and that is unproductive.

My mom told me that if you give someone enough rope, they will hang themselves. This is a lesson you have to learn early in toxic environments. People who have ill will toward you will ultimately lose. Stay true to your values, character, and the facts. Do not get in your feelings when responding, as emotions will get the best of you each and every time. Lastly, what Ice Queen taught us all is do not let things fester, as it only makes you sour. And you will end up being best described by the infamous words of Dr. Seuss of The Grinch…"stink, stank, stunk!"

9 STRANGE CASE OF DR. JEKYLL AND MR. HYDE

The battle of good versus evil can be traced back to the beginning of time. The spiritual tug of war between the two sides has been the cornerstone of stories told in religion, Greek mythology, science fiction, comic warfare, and played out in many plots of theatrical, cinema, and television genres. The concept that light and darkness cannot peacefully coexist but only one can reign, extends far beyond dimensional realms.

Good and evil is a constant internal conflict represented in our individual struggles to decide between right and wrong, which eventually plays out in our interactions with others. The biggest showdown between the two extremes often marks a commencement; the ending of a reign and the start of a new regime. This clash of the titans type battle never results in a true winner, as the outcome of war leaves mutual devastation in the form of scars, casualties, and ruins. The victor has only a few moments of time to enjoy the benefits of their triumph before the opponent resurfaces with a plot to rule.

In the *Strange Case of Dr. Jekyll and Mr. Hyde*, a classic 19th century gothic horror, the concept of dualism within an individual is exemplified. The internal conflict of good versus evil is demonstrated in the main character, Dr. Jekyll, whose suppressed evil desires manifest into an alter ego Mr. Hyde, who creates heinous crimes. It begins with Dr. Jekyll taking a potion to transform into Mr. Hyde, until eventually the transformation becomes involuntary (without the need for the potion) as Hyde overpowers Jekyll.

Duality exists in all of us. As human beings we will have constant battles with two ends of the spectrum, right and wrong, good and evil, and the list continues. It can be argued everyone is inherently good but it is how we choose to handle life experiences and environments and how we manage our behavior, which will determine the winning side.

In my experience in toxic environments, I have had my share of battles between being proactive and reactive in response to the toxicity thrown my way. In this book, you bear witness to my struggles with dealing with the insane behaviors of my colleagues. Ephesians tells us our fight is not with the visible but the invisible principalities, powers, and rulers of darkness. It is with this belief I am able to separate the two. I understand it is not the person but the internal struggles they are facing that are portrayed in their toxic behavior. When you have decided to choose good and sanity within yourself, you are able to survive the insanity and evilness that dwells among you, represented through the human beings with whom you voluntarily and involuntarily interact.

The Final Act

My last act at The Circus ranks as one of the most trying yet climatic times in my life. I thought I had begun to reach my breaking point when the associate director yelled for me to leave his office because I questioned his decision in giving my $30 per item promotional materials to some random eighth graders who had visited the office. I wrote a complaint to The Ringmaster as I was tired, sick and tired of surviving in the environment. Little did I know, what was to come would break me down to tears and start the beginning to my end.

The Circus had recently received a new president who was on a rampage and The Ringmaster, a senior vice president, was on his radar. Regardless of the multitude of positive work he had done for the department he was essentially relieved of his duties. I believe he too had reached his breaking point with the president, as the reasoning for his removal was in regards to some negative remarks he made about the new leadership.

In The Ringmaster's absence as Sr. VP, he was replaced with a 75 year old woman with an accounting background who quickly appointed a companion as assistant executive director. The two banded together to publicly degrade The Ringmaster when he was vice president and as a result were now in his shoes. The problem was the two were clueless to running a department and too prideful to accept help. They were attached at the hip, the blind leading the blind, and in their attempts to do "good" they were evil and destruction was their outcome. Their duplicitous nature represented a dualism of the distortion of right and wrong; thus, I refer to them as Dr. Jerkyll and Mr. Hyde.

First day as interim Sr. VP, Dr. Jekyll came in ready to dismantle The Ringmaster's office and Danille was first on her list. She had a personal vendetta against Danille from several previous encounters when she was just an accounting staff member and it was clear the two of them did not like each other. Many staff from different offices frequented our office suite to warn us about Dr. Jekyll's warpath. They even went to The Ringmaster, who was now transitioning to a lower ranked position, to watch after Danille because Dr. Jekyll had mentioned she was going to fire her. However, she soon would direct her efforts to me, finding out that firing Danille, who handles the budget, would work in the adverse. Essentially, I became the subject of her abuse.

Dr. Jekyll was insane and suffered from memory loss. This is a lady who in a previous year sent an email to everyone in the department informing them to be aware if they were "targeted by The Ringmaster" for attending a retirement ceremony because of a prior disagreement she, personally, had with him. She hadn't been in a leadership position since the Prohibition and absolutely had no clue of how to function in a leadership role in the 21st century. As interim Sr. VP, you would think her focus would have been on just maintaining the position until a permanent vice president was hired. However, she couldn't even fake it until she made it. She focused all her time and energy on me and not the elements of the department. It was told to me that she thought I was going to sabotage her, since I had the closest relationship with The Ringmaster.

This is where having an allegiance can backfire. Sometimes the folks you align with can cause you to be a target strictly based on association, especially when one person of the group is not liked. Shunning, ostracism, bullying, and isolation are all unfortunate results where one is purposefully outcasted, socially punished, emotionally abused, and exiled, respectively. All of which I experienced in this chapter.

Harassment

The saga begins with Dr. Jekyll calling me for meetings and each time changing my job duties and then calling me for another meeting to discuss why I hadn't done the job she had told me to stop doing. As a result, I would eventually send a complaint to human resources (HR) because her antics were nothing short of harassment and a hostile work environment. She moved my office from The Ringmaster's office suite on the third floor to the second floor with the reasoning being she wanted me to help with the entrepreneurial center, which, unbeknownst to her, had been unfunded, unstaffed, and inoperative for over a year.

She would then call me several times a day for the mere purpose of ensuring I was in my office. The phone conversations would go as follows, each time:

Me: This is Porscha

Dr. Jekyll: Yes, Miss Jackson I was just making sure you were in your office.

Me: I'm here. Is someone looking for me?

Dr. Jekyll: No, I just wanted to make sure you were in the office and nowhere else.

Me: Ok

Dr. Jekyll: Good Bye

She would even do pop-up visits and come down to the second floor just to make sure I was sitting in my office. When she would come to the office, she would have nothing to say or to give me. If she had doubts about me not reporting to work, then why move me from the same office suite where you occupy an office to a dormant office suite on the second floor?   If I had remained in my third floor office, she would have known exactly when and where I was because I would have had to walk past her office to get to mine.

Then she stopped conducting office visits to me by herself and started to bring along her minion, Mr. Hyde.   Imagine my day of being constantly interrupted with check-in calls as if I am on parole.   Then having to see the likes of Dr. Jekyll, a six foot, thin woman dressed in a 1980's masculine suit hanging off her body with a thinly strand salt and peppered hair styled from foam rollers, gold thin-rimmed square glasses on her sunken facial features and tan Jesus sandals. Mr. Hyde was a late 40's early 50's 5 '6, medium-build, short-legged, fast walking, clean cut brown complexioned know-it-all with dark spots on his face like a leopard.   Now, I have two people, who are running the department, taking time out of their day to walk down two flights of stairs just to see if I am sitting in my office. I must be someone special!

One day Dr. Jekyll called me and I did not answer the phone because I had gone to the restroom.   Angry that I did not answer, she sent me an email and told me I must answer the phone each and every time she called.   I explained to her that my job duties sometimes require me to take things to other buildings on company campus and go to meetings throughout the building and other buildings; in addition, I do leave my desk to go to the restroom and heat my lunch in the breakroom.   Next thing I know, she called to tell me that each time I went to the restroom I would need to record when I went and returned on a sheet of paper in her office suite.   I asked why I would do such a thing, especially when there is a restroom on the second floor.   What would be the purpose for me traveling to the third floor to document I was going to the restroom?   She said because I was a part of her office and she needed to keep account of where everyone was at all times.   I reiterated to her that moving me to the second floor, changing my job duties, and giving me a supervisor was a result of removing me from her office. I also asked if she had informed the rest of the people who were actually in her office and directly reported to her that they had to sign in and out for the restroom...she said "no, why would I do that?"...exactly, then you won't do that with me and I never abided by her restroom rule.

Controls and Isolations

Dr. Jekyll's intent was to isolate me in order to control me. This is a tactic commonly used in abusive and other oppressive situations. Dr. Jekyll was more than likely threatened by me, hence her idea that I had plans to sabotage her though she was better capable of that than I.   If she could separate me from the others in the office, she could render me powerless by painting me as being a negative person, dismantling any allies I had, and terminating me.

Earlier on, she sent an email to about 10 people, including myself, which stated my new supervisor, new duties, and The Ringmaster as my "coach/mentor/trainer". Confused as to why I was the only person on the list to have a coach/mentor/trainer, I asked for clarification. Mr. Hyde responded that it was because The Ringmaster and I were close. This was one of the early signs I was being targeted for no apparent reason, even to Mr. Hyde, based on his response.

Then Dr. Jekyll, daily, began to take main job duties away from me, especially those of authoritative leadership. She told me one day that she was assigning the website content to the director of instructional technology. I communicated to her my disagreement with the move as I was the director of public relations and it would be awkward to have the IT director manage website content as it involved writing and branding, something I was the only person working on those aspects. Jekyll just sat there and looked at me and later told me she would "think about it". It was clear she was not thinking about anything but stripping me of authority.

Her next move was assigning public relations tasks to Militia, who was antisocial, militant, sexist (towards women), outdated, rude, and abrasive. There was a request for an ad from the department and Jekyll assigned it to Militia who submitted an ad in the design of a certificate which included an outdated company mantra. The ad looked like something from the 1990's; actually, it had to be from the 90's because the mantra was last used during that decade. Furthermore, it took her two days to figure out how to make the file in landscape and not portrait. Clearly, Jekyll did not need me to sabotage her, she was doing that by taking the department back in time. She knew she was out of her league but to disguise her ignorance she chose to revert everything back to a time that no longer existed.

There were a multitude of complaints from people inside and outside of our department of branding from that ad which was featured in a booklet for a major event in the city. The irony was all things came to light. The same staff members who were behind her in her attempt to bring The Ringmaster down, treated her very differently after that, not sure if they saw her for the joke she was but I know they did see her as a mistake in the role of interim vice president.

After a few months of her control tactics, I asked her to explain my job duties because she kept changing them and holding me responsible for the ones she took from me. She responded slowly, pausing after each word "I don't know" as if I was slow to comprehend. She then changed the subject and asked me about information in emails that were not sent to me and then insisted these emails were indeed sent to me after I asked her to pull them up and show me where my email address was listed in said emails. Her sent files did not show she had sent any of the emails in question to me, so she told me to check my inbox because the emails were there.

I had finally had enough. I made a complaint to HR about Dr. Jekyll's shenanigans in addition to the ones below.

- She continued to eliminate and alter my job duties without explanation.

- She gave the production of website content responsibility to the Director of IT. When I brought it to her attention it was my responsibility, she responded that she didn't know I was in charge of it. Despite receiving a list of my duties at her request a few days after she assumed the interim Sr. VP position.

- I handled an event that was in progress before she came into office. I asked her if she wanted me to continue with it and she said yes. Then she started doing the same thing I was doing and it caused confusion among other company offices as she was not managing the process correctly.

- She took away my subordinates without explanation and reason.

- She would give me an organizational chart that had me in charge of a center (that was unfunded and inoperative) but told me verbally that my responsibilities were not of the center but to answer questions when people visited this center. I then asked that my name be removed because the verbal duties needed to correlate with what was documented in writing as to be consistent with expectations. I was given the response that I needed to check with my supervisor; I did and he said he had no work for me to do because the center was inoperable.

- October 13 I asked that she put my job duties in writing and she refused. She asked my new supervisor about my duties and he said he would get back to me. When he did, he said he had no idea she was going to ask him that, especially because he has no duties for me because the center is inoperable.

- Nov 18th she sent an email that my job duty of doing departmental payroll timesheets was being removed from me to a temporary receptionist that was hired three days prior. I asked her if I did anything wrong as she would take this duty from me and give it to someone who has no experience. Dr. Jekyll said that she "didn't know if [I] did anything wrong" and that she would let me know next week. She originally said I didn't give instructors enough time to sign their timesheet and I explained that I gave the time frame based on the company's mandated time frame to process payroll in a timely manner to ensure all department staff were paid on time. Danille was my witness in this meeting as she spoke up several times about emails Jekyll had sent to her (Danille) and not me but Jekyll would chastise me for it anyway.

- She claimed I needed to copy her on any email that may affect her. I questioned where the line would be drawn because the argument could be made that everything could affect her eventually. She replied "I'll let you be the judge. If anything you send to someone gets back to me and you didn't copy me, then I will document it."

- Dr. Jekyll came into my office and pointed her fingers towards my eyes, in the motion of poking them out, to ask me where I was when she called me five minutes prior and I did not answer the phone.
- Dr. Jekyll and Mr. Hyde came to my office on the second floor to ask me if I received an email she sent to six people and copied me on.

Jekyll's controlling ways would even flow into who, when, and where I could go on company campus. I remember Jekyll telling me I had to get permission from her when I could walk across campus and if permission was granted, I could not walk with Danille.   Mr. Hyde said I was observed "following [Danille]" and because of that it seemed that "I had no work to do".   Offended he would imply I was "following" someone upsetted me. I told him that "I do not follow anyone" and when I go to another building, alone or in company, it is work related. Additionally, I had observed him too but it was clear he was indeed "following Dr. Jekyll across the campus" because he had no invites to the meetings she was attending.

Their accusations were so petty and juvenile. I further explained Danille and I were also walking to other buildings together as a safety precaution mandated by company security who sent an email to walk in pairs due to recent crime in the neighborhood. I pointed out to Jekyll that other staff walked together even when they were not going for work purposes and that even she and Mr. Hyde walked together, so if she is not imposing the same rules on other staff, then she could not single me out. She gave me a glare and said nothing.

Bullying

I guess *what was good for the goose, was good for the gander* and "ain't no fun if the homies can't have none" were the mottos Dr. Jekyll lived by, as she began to enlist her work friends to harass me as well. Dr. War was notorious for harassing people, including visitors, clients, staff, birds, bugs, gnats, and whoever and whatever looked better than her. She was probably the most decorated trainer in our department with the most claims filed against her of all sorts.   Participants had literally threatened her life because of malicious things she said to them because of their complexion, hair styles, clothes, and place of origin. She told a staff member her clothes were "too tight", told participants they wouldn't get jobs, and called an intern "a thug", and declared 'no one would ever hire him', all in public settings, which caused her to lose her position as a lead trainer.

It was a simple and sad case of oppressing the oppressor, where the wounded found gratification in inflicting the same measure of pain they had received from being bullied. Dr. War was the same person, who emotionally broke down one day about her struggle with being a dark-skinned black woman who was called "ugly" and teased about having "nappy hair" as a child.   The failure of her same race peers to accept her because of her physicality was an everlasting scar to her self-esteem. In her breakdown, she said receiving a doctorate degree was her way of proving she was smart to anyone in her past, present, and future. However, she used the doctorate as a weapon to degrade others who reminded her of those she never gained acceptance. This was clearly a tactic of relational aggression.

As a program participant, prior to my full time employment at The Circus, I felt the wrath of her insecurities. At a business competition meeting, she randomly walked over to me and commented that she thought my blue nails were "ugly". With all eyes on her and ears attentive to the situation, before she could get anything else out, another participant spoke up and said "I think her nails are beautiful. Why would you say something like that? They are not chipped and they're manicured." She responded "That's right, it's my opinion and I think they are ugly and they are too long. I don't care if they are manicured." I then replied "You're right, you have your opinion. I didn't paint my nails for you, so not sure why you even expressed it. You don't like my nails, so what. I think we are here to talk about business plans." *My question was, what mid-fifty year old woman does this to 20 year old program participants?*

It was obvious that pretty discrimination in the form of lookism had reared its ugly head yet again. Dr. War was abusive and was a consistent offender to those she thought were attractive. She sought to belittle and shame them solely on their physical appearance; additionally, she was no respecter of persons. Whether it was participants, interns, or staff, you could count on her to make an inappropriately aggressive comment about their appearance. As time went on, she would try to make the same petty comments about things I would wear and I would just be dismissive as I was before and she eventually stopped.

That's how you have to be with people who are looking to pick a fight. This was her way of getting attention. These types of personalities like attention whether it is positive or negative, either way, if you engage them then it's attention and they want it. When you ignore them, they can't function, so they will say anything to get a rise out of you because then you become focused on them. When you have narcissists like this, pay them no attention and move on as if they do not exist. If you must engage them, keep your answers short, factual and to the point as if not to leave room for their comments because they will try their best to suck you in to suffer in misery with them. They're in a constant war within themselves and as the saying goes, *misery loves company.*

Now with Dr. Jekyll as interim, Dr. War decided to rekindle our encounter from years prior. She sent me an email, with sarcastic undertones and Dr. Jekyll and Mr. Hyde copied, asking why I had not promoted a professional development conference, specifically for departmental trainers and staff, in a newsletter geared towards the current program participants and program alumni. I responded, as I just told you, short and factually, pointing out the targeted market of the newsletter would not be qualified to attend the conference, so advertising an event to a population who was prohibited from attending would be meaningless and a waste of time. It was a few other senseless petty gestures she would do to bully me publicly and via email. Each time, it was based on interactions and information stemmed from an email sent to me from Jekyll.

Spitefulness

I have never been around so many childish and amateur professionals in my life. All they had was spite which fueled their actions and interactions while providing a contentious comfort. There was not a plan to ratify all the misdoings they accused The Ringmaster of committing. They were simply focused on dethroning him that they had not considered even the smallest plan should their heist work.

When Dr. Jekyll first assumed her role as interim vice president, there was a dinner scheduled for the online executive leadership program participants. Ironically, neither Jekyll, Mr. Hyde, nor Dr. Harlequin, the director of the program, had any clue of how to conduct themselves at a banquet. Here I was thinking, *you three could not wait to get The Ringmaster out because you felt he was doing so poorly and as soon as you step into office, you have no plan?* I guess I gave them too much credit.

Needless to say, I had to run the banquet. I had to host, run the check-in table, MC, take pictures, and plan and execute the entire event by myself. Dr. Harlequin did not even know how to make remarks during the program. If you cannot make remarks or engage with participants who are enrolled in the program that you lead, then that truly shows how unqualified you are for the position. Additionally, Dr. Jekyll and Mr. Hyde did not even make any remarks when prompted. They must have watched an episode of the Three Stooges before attending the banquet as they were pointing at each other like Larry, Moe and Curly to decide who would come to the podium and address these professional participants whose tuition brought in more money than any other training program in our department. Eventually, all three made an on-the-spot agreement on who would make the remarks. From his seat, Dr. Harlequin pointed to me, as I was standing at the podium after introducing the executive team of stooges, and said "you go ahead and make the remarks".

Having to turn the banquet into a one-woman show, I thought that making the closing remarks at the request of the stooges was most baffling. However, in retrospect, the most baffling was the giraffe outfit Dr. Jekyll wore. She, at 6 feet, wore a giraffe print shirt with 1980's Dynasty inspired shoulder pads and a giraffe print scarf hat to match. It was not only outdated by several decades but it was ugly and old. It looked like she purchased it in the early 80's not only because of the style but the discoloration and upkeep of the fabric. Picture wearing a giraffe rug as a blouse with pants to match. It was probably the only laughter I had that night, nearly in tears when she walked through the door to a business professional attire banquet. This was another moment, *you had to see it to believe it.* I took a picture with every intent of putting it wherever I could, so others could enjoy a good laugh too. After all, everyone comes to the circus to see the animals.

It was a shame that I had to do the entire event with no help because Jekyll and Hyde had taken away my assistant, with the belief I did not have a large enough workload to share, when I had more work assignments than anyone in that entire office. My assistant, ironically, was reassigned to Mr Hyde. However, she kept coming to me for work as Hyde had absolutely nothing for her to do. I gave her work at her request under the disclaimer she needed to obey their rules as she no longer worked for me. Well Jekyll and Hyde found out she was helping me and got on my case, which is how I was left without an attendant for the check-in table at the banquet.

I originally thought it was their plan to isolate me and take away all of my responsibilities so they could claim I was underperforming as a reason for termination. That's where documentation took place, yet again. I forced Jekyll to send emails to me, so I could build a case against her and when she would call me up stairs for meetings, I would document everything: the time, who was in the meetings, and what everyone wore and said. My short hand was on point.

Petty Emails

Dr. Jekyll would start petty arguments via email. She would accuse me of not being in the office even though I would send her notices when I was leaving to attend the golf lessons the department sponsored for our upcoming tournament. She blamed me for not copying her on emails for events and emails that took place months before she was interim. She told Danille that "if you said it, then I believe it" and accused me of sending emails that I didn't send. When I asked for proof of the emails she claimed I sent, she said she had to look for them. If it was such a mistake that I committed, then she should definitely have proof and know exactly what emails she was referencing.

I found it so disturbing she would make bold accusations without any proof. The burden of proof is on the plaintiff and without proof, it's false allegations. She would even go as far as to tell me to check my sent files of the emails she claimed I sent and when I sent her a screenshot of my sent files, she claimed I deleted the emails. The same emails she could not find in her inbox from me. It was later revealed in meetings that someone else had sent her the emails and she thought I sent them, that is why she could never find them under my name. She never once apologized for the mistakes and name calling. When the person(s) brought it to her attention the emails came from them and not me, she just said "oh".

The whole situation with Dr. Jekyll was ridiculous. She had told me I needed to respond to every email she sent me, regardless if it garnered a response or not. It had even gotten to a point where she said I needed to copy at least two other people on any email I sent to her. This mandate was a result of me sending her an email that she never responded to but then claimed I had not sent the email. However, I provided proof that I indeed sent her the email. She then, of course, shifted the blame to me saying that anytime I sent her an email those other folks needed to be copied. I had seriously gotten tired of her trying to paint me out as a liar, which is the polar opposite of who I am, and she knew it. She was just trying to discredit me; however, my work spoke for itself because to whom she told that I "was no good" defended me and said they had never experienced what she said of me in all their years of knowing me. That made her angry. Additionally, the same folks doted on how good of a worker I was and how they enjoyed working with me. She was even upset when another company director expressed his desire for me to work in his office.

People were used to and enjoyed working with me and that was evident because they continued, even on things she was trying to handle. These folks would call and tell me they had requested things from her and had yet to receive them, so they were calling me for assistance. These were directors and executives of The Circus. Once she got wind of this, she accused me of going behind her back to sabotage her. It's ironic because she was trying to sabotage me but did not even consider the same folks she was defaming me to were informing me of what she was saying about me. I explained these people had contacted me on their own free will and I just responded. She didn't believe that because her intent was to destroy me. I thought I would react in the same way but it was not in my heart. I just wanted to do my job peacefully but she had convinced herself that I had ill intent; in psychology, this term is called projection.

Setback is Set Up for a Comeback

I must admit, the treatment they gave me did break me down for a spell. It just came out of nowhere and I felt defeated and helpless. I tried going to HR for assistance, all to find out it was a disingenuous effort. The things the HR officer told me to do, I had already done and no resolve came from their guidance. They spoke with Dr. Jekyll and advised her to have witnesses in the room anytime she met with me, but told me that she was in her right to give my job duties and staff to others without reason; require me to stay in my office and notify her of my restroom breaks, as long as I was not being singled out; subject me to her ridiculous email, phone, and office rules; bully and berate me to others; and threaten me with gestures, just as long as she did not touch me. After meeting with HR, I left thinking they were in cahoots with Dr. Jekyll because I knew I was being harassed, I had proof of a hostile work environment, but yet I was being told to keep to myself and perform whatever duties I was assigned, even if it changed frequently.

The constant microscope and mistreatment weighed heavily on me. People who once looked up to me, now pitied me. It seemed as if I had invisible shackles on my limbs; I could see them but they were invisible to others, so no one knew I was caged. When you have no one to turn to at work that can help you, it hurts. When your superiors are the ones shackling you and HR is not advocating for policy on your behalf, resolve seems bleak.

It eventually takes a toll when you know you have done nothing wrong and tried to abide by the rules and the environment gets worse. I remember sitting in my office in tears after getting off a phone call where Dr. Jekyll had again berated me for something I did not do. I heard a knock at my office door but I did not make a sound, hoping whoever it was would just go away. Then I saw the door knob twist, I immediately began to wipe my tears, thinking it was Dr. Jekyll as only a few people had a key that would unlock my door, but it was Danille. She had come to check on me as she knew what I was going through and thought I was not answering the door to avoid Jekyll and Hyde.

Later that day, I remembered my church was having a prayer conference and all the years I had attended the church, I never went to this annual event. I was at the end of the rope; I did not know what else to do. I thought about the lady with the issue of blood in the Bible, who pressed her way through the crowd just to touch the hem of Jesus' garment. I believed she just needed a glimpse of hope, to do something that would comfort her faith. I likened our helpless situations and decided to press my way to Jesus because maybe if I just showed up in his presence, as broken as I was, just maybe I could be made whole again.

I arrived about an hour late and quietly found a seat in the back. That night in the back of the church, I cried as I heard the first lady give a scripture about how we have to love our enemies and those who despitefully persecute us because we have the upper hand. She encouraged all in attendance to not allow those who mistreat us to discourage us because they were already defeated. As she began to preach more, my seat moved closer and the thousands of people disappeared and I was the only one in the room and she was now speaking directly to me. That night, I left the church with confidence in knowing God had the final word and if He was for me, then anyone against me had already failed. My sorrow breathed life into their actions, so if I wanted to reclaim my happiness, I had to start believing I was the victor.

A few days later, I spoke with a long-time friend over the phone and unloaded about my situation. The church conference had given me the confidence to boldly talk about my experience without feeling ashamed or defeated. It was hard because people knew me for being courageous and strong and excellent at my job. I would always be the one to uplift others and tell them what to do on their job because I had been in bad work environments before and was thriving in one but this time it had gotten the best of me. I told my friend what was happening and she encouraged me to continue to be me, to look for employment elsewhere, and to not back down to anything they said. "Don't let them win!" she declared. She then reminded me of how talented I was and what I had accomplished and to not let that go to waste due to the vindictiveness of Jekyll and her minions. She reminded me nothing lasts forever and this situation was only temporary. After our phone call, I felt even more empowered to not let their actions destroy me.

Redemption Tour

There was yet another meeting with me to discuss a change in my job duties. This time was different. I was no longer letting their toxic behavior consume me. Jekyll had tried to tear me down with the usual pointing out things I did not do right, that were not my responsibility or that I flat out did not do because another person did it and I was being blamed, regardless. It was like no matter what I said, she was not going to believe it, so why argue. I just let her be wrong and chose not to help her, so she could embarrass herself by herself.

Every time she called me into her meaningless meetings, I would just sit there and not give her any eye contact and would just take shorthand notes for my documentation. Unbothered is what she got from me and it worked. When she began to accuse me of something, I would just interrupt her and say "that wasn't me, couldn't have been me because I was [wherever I was at that time]" or "remember you told me at the last meeting on [such and such date] that I was no longer over it, so I obeyed your wishes so that is why it wasn't done".

She would then get angry and start stuttering and would say to me "if I told you to do something you need to do it". Then I would refute and say "exactly, that's why I didn't do it because you told me not to. Had you not taken that responsibility from me on [such and such date], that would have been something that I automatically would have done but when you assigned it to someone else, it was no longer my responsibility it was theirs...do you need to call them in to tell them how they didn't do THEIR job, how they didn't do what YOU told them to do or are YOU just going to blame me for everything that goes wrong?". That was my one two punch everytime to get her off my case; especially, because with each meeting she started inviting more random people to come for what seemed the purpose of ridiculing me. I now felt the sentiments of the tamed lion in the circus. My new found confidence and reassured faith flipped her act because I was no longer performing under her command.

Game Recognized

The funny part was it would take Jekyll three good roastings before she devised another plan. Her public roasts of me became too much and began to work adversely. One of the facilitators she invited to one of the meetings caught me in the hallway alone and said "why does she treat you so badly?" I responded, "she always does that. I'm used to it." He said, "I'm sorry, I didn't know she had invited me to a meeting just for that. There was no purpose in my being there and it was a complete waste of my time. If she happens to do that again when I'm in a meeting, I will stick up for you because that was ridiculous and unwarranted." I appreciated what he said because it was true and it is always good when someone who is not your friend sees the unjust and speaks up. My shackles were now becoming visible, even though I had already mentally freed myself. I really wished he would have said something at the meeting, in front of them, in front of everyone, but my mojo was working and if I was going down, I was going guns blazing!

Afterglow

After Jekyll's third attempt to embarrass me backfired, she allowed her minions to do the dirty work as she sat back in the meeting and said nothing. The third attempt was actually funny because HR had told her she needed another manager besides her sidekick, Hyde, in the room when she spoke to me. She invited the Neutralist, from the puppetry who was so neutral she might as well have been a mummy. She was basically a nonfactor, she said nothing, spoke up for nothing, and as far as I know did nothing.

Like the others, Jekyll came with her same ol' 'you didn't do this, didn't do that and last time I told you that you were to do what I said even if it was no longer your job duty…'. I simply said, "You don't remember you said you were going to handle the situation? I would think as a VP, you would want to contact that person because you told me not to have any communication with them anymore, even if they contacted me instead of you. Maybe you should check that little book you always write things down in. Go ahead, I'll wait… You don't see it in there? You didn't record it?" The Neutralist burst out laughing as Jekyll was feverishly flipping through the pages of her flowered journal trying to find it. She was nervous and Hyde was encouraging her, "yeah you wrote it down, keep looking in your book". Comical. She could not find it and now embarrassed, she said when she has "some time", she would look for it and let me know. I said "Well, when you find it, be sure to let me know what YOU wrote." Her glare sent beams through my eyes, farther than her boney fingers could when she pointed them at me in my office.

Not having had enough, she argued with the same tired tactic of putting all the responsibility on me, instead of taking accountability as the interim vice president for her actions. She told me, *regardless of whether or not she told me to do something, if I know it has to be done, I am responsible for doing it.* What am I to do? She basically described that no matter what I did, I was going to be in trouble, a perfect Catch 22…damned if I do and damned if I don't. Well, I guess I don't because it wastes my time if I do.

I repeated what she said "so you want me to be responsible for the responsibilities you gave me and the responsibilities of others?" She said "yes", then I replied "so have you shared this with others as well or am I the only one you have these demands on because last time you brought me up here, you told me I don't report to you, so maybe you need to contact HR before you go changing my job duties again." Her silence was golden. For some reason, she thought I was oblivious to her speaking with HR after they spoke to her about me speaking to them.

The Neutralist's eyes got big and she began to shake her head and Hyde was looking in confusion back at Jekyll as she was dumbfounded with her wrinkled hands on her journal book and said "Well I guess that's the right thing to do." I then gathered my papers and said "is there anything else?", she said "no" and I got up and walked out and it sounded like cold silence. I knew they couldn't wait for me to get out of that room so they could talk about me. It was a new day and I walked out of that office with my head held high and a stride in my step. I had gotten her off my back for a couple of weeks. Then she concocted another plan, which was when her minions took control.

Dr. Harlequin started his charge towards me by sending an email blaming me for not doing my "job". He sent an email and copied four people saying that Ms. Sam was waiting on me to do a flyer and I was not performing my job duties by not providing him status on Ms. Sam's request. He added I had not approved information to be sent to the IT director for placement on the screens. *Here we go with the television screens, again.* I informed him that not only had the information been approved by Mr. B, the approving authority of flyers, but it was sent to the computing manager for placement on the screens as the director of IT does not do screen placement. Again, Dr. Harlequin showed that he had no clue of what was going on.

Needless to say, Dr. Harlequin was pissed because not only did I know he was clueless but so did the four people he decided to copy to try to embarass me. Furthermore, Dr. Jekyll forgot to inform Harlequin that in an effort to strip me of my authority, she assigned all content approval to Mr. B, whom he was afraid to confront. Dr. Harlequin prior to the Jekyll and Hyde reign, had been viewed as a nuisance by staff but I was the only person who would carry on a full fledged conversation with him without spearing insults. He wanted power and knowing he would have to speak to Mr. B and the computing manager, who did not like him either, the future did not look so bright anymore. His plan foiled and it was really sad because Dr. Harlequin and I never had a problem before. In fact, he used to bring me gifts from India when The Ringmaster was Sr. VP, in addition to the talks about his family and other conversations we would have. The things people do for a chance at power.

The interesting part of his "social climb" was he picked the wrong ladder. Word was Jekyll and Hyde had done so much damage in so little time, the company president was putting a rush on finding a permanent VP. The dynamic duo had made quite a name for themselves as the new Circus act of "Dumb and Dumber". The president frequently complained publicly that Jekyll had created a mess with her destructive ways which brought negative attention to the department by ruining external partner relations and unraveling the programs The Ringmaster had established. The president's original intent was for Jekyll to keep the department afloat until a permanent VP was hired. She went to meetings and all she had to do was be quiet but she would speak up and her lack of knowledge would speak volumes. Then she, being accompanied by Mr. Hyde at all meetings and events, enacted the president to go on a rant about how associate directors should not attend every meeting with vice presidents.

They became a running joke among company staff, with people constantly asking "What is wrong with your department?" and the president regretting his decision of placing her as interim. The irony, yet again, was whatever Jekyll tried to do to me ended up happening to her. In her attempt to eliminate me from executive sessions (on her claim that I was planning to sabotage her), I was being asked to serve on more company-wide executive committees, where she was the topic of discussion on ignorance.

The last meeting I was called for was so ridiculous and her obvious intent to shame me vicariously through her minion Dr. Harlequin, was an epic fail. She egged him on in the meeting about a flyer that was made and how it did not feature any of our program participants and how I had not consulted with him on the final draft. Keeping with tradition, Jekyll had invited the Neutralist and another staffer to hear Harlequin repeatedly talk about the flyers. I simply informed him the flyers were the same flyers we had used last year and they were a reorder.

He didn't have a problem with the flyers last year, so I wasn't understanding the sudden change of opinion. He started stuttering and then Hyde slid the flyers to me because I said, "what are you talking about" as I had been called to the meeting under the pretense I was coming to address "a girl who had internship questions", even though I was no longer over any programs or interns. Those were Jekyll's exact words, but when I got to the third floor, there was no girl but Jekyll, Neutralist, Hyde, Harlequin, and Ms. Sam were there and the women in that group were far from being classified as "a girl". As soon as I sat down, they started talking about how upset they were about these flyers, so I asked "what flyers?" That's when Hyde slid the flyers to me so hard that it almost hit my forehead and gave me a papercut.

I was fed up. I let Dr. Harlequin have a piece of my mind. I told him "how can you bring me up here saying that you needed me to answer a question about internships for a "girl" and there is no girl here. Was this a trick? Then you are going to throw some flyers in my face as if I know what you are talking about?" Then Jekyll jumps in to clarify and says "yes I wanted you to answer a question for Ms. Sam". *Since when is a woman in her late 40's a girl?* Then Hyde apologizes for the near papercut as Harlequin goes on about how I should have contacted him for the flyers, included our program participants on the flyers, and conducted a photoshoot for the pictures. I flipped the script and then began to point out that the flyers in question were the same ones he raved about last year and it was just a reorder because he indicated he needed some immediately for an event later on that week. I went on stating I was still the director of public relations, as my reordering authority had not been transferred to someone else. All that was needed was an approval from Jekyll, which she gave, "so maybe you need to take the issue up with her instead of me".

Secondly, "if you want to use our participants and want a professional photoshoot, then have you decided which participants? Do you have a budget for the photoshoot? Do you have the budget for a professional photographer? Have you gotten this approved by the company as they have guidelines regarding the use of program participant images for public documents?" He said "well no, that would be your job." *Then if it is my job, then why is it a point of discussion? If it is my job then this meeting is irrelevant and so are his opinions.* I continued "So what you all need to do is make up your minds on what you want my job description to be and until you do, I will continue to perform my job duties as stated by the description given to HR and the next time you invite me to a meeting, you need to send me an email and a description of what it is about and not have me here on false pretenses and have the HR representative here as well because that is what they told me to tell you. Is there anything else?" Jekyll replied, "no and I thank you for clearing up the intern issue." I exited again with my confident stride.

Later on Danille asked "who were you letting have it? I had to come and shut the doors because we were like, *whoever they got in there is giving it to them.*" She said Dr. Harlequin was stuttering and left the suite mad and Jekyll did nothing. I told her, it was me and I had had it with them bullying me. The next week, I would get an email telling me to move to the first floor and work in another office under Ms. Womack.

Last Move

My final office at The Circus was with the guest relations office, where they pretty much left me alone for the most part, except when they wanted something done they did not want to do themselves because it had been reassigned by Jekyll. For some reason, she did not understand that if you take away my job duties, you have to give them to someone else to do, they just don't disappear. When Jekyll would give my job duties away, she would say that I was no longer to be involved with it and needed to surrender all of the files immediately to her office and she'd 'figure it out'. I did, but everytime they would have the temporary administrative assistant ask me to explain the files, which I had already done in an email sent to them.

They wanted me to surrender the files and then tell them what was in the files and then train the person who they had not told was taking over the task on what to do. How can I train the person to do something and you haven't even told me or the person that they are doing it? One example was when Jekyll told me to relinquish all of the intern files to Neutralist, who didn't want to communicate with any of the interns. She often would send their concerns to me instead of handling them. In these particular situations, you have to become proactive and stay two steps ahead of them. The Neutralist tried to send some disgruntled interns to me but I was happy to send them back to her office with the message that I am no longer over internships nor was I responsible for interns. The Neutralist was in charge and I had been instructed not to handle any matters that did not involve my job description.

I was done because they did the same thing continuously out of redundancy. The Neutralist was mad but what could she do? She had sided with the devil and never spoke up for me when she knew I was being falsely accused of things because she had done some of them. My fed up-o-meter was overflowing as I had become immune to their attacks and apathetic to their feelings. In what would be my last act with The Circus, I fell into the traps of most disengaged employees. I arrived late, took long lunches and breaks, and mentally checked out. Since I was stripped of most of my responsibilities, I did about a half of a day's work, so when Neutralist wanted help with her new internship managerial role, I provided no assistance at all. You did not speak up for me when I was getting clobbered, so I just merely returned the favor, especially because if I was not in charge of something, I was not supposed to be involved.

The Lesson

There are no true happy endings in toxic environments. Either you stay and eventually succumb to your injuries or you walk away with scars. It would be nice to believe that at some point the environment goes through a detoxification and what was once harmful now breeds health and happiness. The reality is toxicity is a culture composed of jargon, beliefs, habits, customs, knowledge, policies, and behaviors. It is embedded in the fabric of the organization which cannot be discontinued through the magical workshops of human resource professionals, promotions, and department retreats. In fact, it is perpetuated through mediums that guide and shape the organization. Therefore toxicity does not disappear when separated from the source but invisibly lives in those who embrace the culture, no matter where they go and associate.

My experiences under the regime of Dr. Jekyll and Mr. Hyde was a perfect culmination of my lessons learned at The Circus. My documentation of events, ability to stick to the facts and remain calm in hostile situations, decision to not return an eye for an eye, and determination to stand my ground, were all contributions to my survival and misfit. I could not have endured the oppression and abuse without the support of friends, faith, and a sound mind.

Jekyll and Hyde's dualism was an evident struggle we all face, especially in toxic environments. Do we relax who we are to get along or do we take the abuse to remain true to ourselves? It is indeed a fight for the survival of the fittest but the question is, do we really want to survive and are we really a fit? The internal battles between two extremes will never go away but it is how we choose to overcome them within ourselves that determines our external fight. The adoption of the idiom "If you can't beat them, join them" is an acceptance of a mental defeat to stay in an unwanted situation. Are you a part of the culture or not? Ultimately, it is the question you have to ask yourself to define your stance within the toxicity in the environment.

In the Case of Dr. Jekyll and Mr. Hyde, the novel comes to an end when Jekyll succumbs to the evilness of his alter ego, Mr. Hyde. With good losing the internal battle and evil prevailing externally, Jekyll commits suicide as his last good gesture of stopping Hyde's criminal activity. He attempts to gain solace through a letter to his friend, admitting to the crimes, as a result of his dissonance. The novel concluded with the final line of the letter, which read: "Here then, as I lay down the pen and proceed to seal up my confession, I bring the life of that unhappy Henry Jekyll to an end."

The discord we have in toxic environments can be emotionally and mentally harmful to ourselves and others involved. Our struggle with the opposing forces should not end in the tragedy of the novel but should serve as a warning to the power of toxicity and its repercussions. These environments are not to be taken lightly. Though my experience was not deadly, it was an eye opener to the battles people face internally that are exhibited externally on a daily basis. Hurt people, hurt others and you have to choose if you are going to be hurt or well, no matter what happens and no matter what or who is surrounding you. This is when you have to separate the behavior from the person. Had I not done this in the case of Jekyll, Hyde, Dr. War, and Dr. Harlequin, I would have accepted the spirit of defeat and placed blame on them personally, resulting in destructive actions towards them and ultimately destroying myself and my future well being.

The turning point in this chapter was hearing the scripture of Luke 6:27-38 from the first lady at the church conference. In a nutshell, it juxtaposes your desires against your actions. If you want forgiveness, you have to forgive; if you want to escape judgment, then don't judge; and if you expect goodness to come your way, then you must extend it, unconditionally. The most jarring part of the passage is learning to take the high road and not reciprocate behaviors or actions, even in defense. It says to *love your enemies; do good to others when they are not good to you; offer your other cheek when struck; bless them that curse you; and pray for those who mistreat you, for with the same measure you use, it will be measured to you.*

These are tough words to live by but it is a process that epitomizes that two wrongs do not equal right, nor does fighting fire with fire extinguish the flames. What it teaches us is integrity, courage, and strength. It makes us change agents and vessels of light in the midst of darkness by holding us in a higher regard to receive a greater reward. Reciprocating hurt means we will receive the repercussions associated with hurting others; it is nothing but a destructive cycle. There is no reward in being miserable like them, you are greater and you deserve better, so hold your head up high knowing that no matter what, good always prevails in the end.

I speak from the depth of experience and practice the words that I have preached. I thought I could never forgive Jekyll and her minions but soon realized I did not have the energy to harbor ill feelings towards them nor the time to give them any further thought. I remember coming back to the company a year after my departure to give The Ringmaster my taxes (he would do them for me) and Dr. Harlequin ran up to me to hear all about how I was doing in my doctorate program. Apparently, he had asked about me in my absence and The Ringmaster and/or Danille had filled him in, as they were the only two whom I kept in contact with. Harlequin was back to the person he was before the Jekyll and Hyde administration. When I saw him, I did not feel the discomfort I once felt when we had our last interaction. It took prayer and the absorption of the aforementioned scripture to forgive all the hurt and pain they inflicted upon me. I had to realize I was in a better situation now and the minions and their leader were part of a plan to get me to this higher place in life. If it was not for Goliath, David would have not become king.

The end of The Circus marked the end of an era for me. Actually, it was more than a circus, it was a culture that I did not fit into but was divinely a part of. The experiences and lessons it taught me formed the foundation of who I am as a professional woman. It strengthened my character, built my skill set, and prepared me for the cold world. The Circus revealed to me who I was by showing me who I did not want to become. It gave me thick skin and stretched me professionally and emotionally, and for that, I am forever grateful. The performances under The Big Top were unfortunately, not one of a kind, because they can happen in any organization, association, department, group, and family; however, they were not all bad. There were thrills, opportunities, and friendships that I have not experienced anywhere else. The times were good and bad but the toxicity taught me the greatest lesson in life, Don't Ever Lose Sight of Who You Are!

10   DETOX

My feet spread shoulder width apart, focused as I sway my body from side to side, right hip left shoulder then left hip right shoulder, vigorously pumping my arm with my hand in a fist to the air as I picture myself dressed in camouflage singing "I'm a survivor, I'm not gon' give up, I'm not gon' stop, I'm gon' work harder". It is truly amazing how the simplicity of lyrics can capture the complexity of years of experiences in the verses of a three minute song. It is not just the words, it's the feeling in the uniquely different ways each listener is able to personally define the phrases as we connect our pains and joys with lyrics belted out over melodic sounds. Songs are our soundtracks to life and books are our bibles, guiding us, documenting our feelings, and serving as our outlets as we journey through life.

This book is a representation of the mountains I've climbed and valleys I've wallowed through to get to me. My experience is uniquely mine but the principles and lessons are ours. Being fully human is recognizing our life is not our own but that each path taken connects us and each decision affects us and I need you just as much as you need me to survive.

Survival of the fittest is not just about a Darwinian concept of natural selection that only the strongest species survive on earth. It applies to the concept of whether or not one is able to survive in a particular work environment. I, just like many of you, was able to survive and some of you are still surviving in toxic work environments, but it does not necessarily constitute whether you are a fit for the environment. Sometimes you survive just to stay alive and that is exactly what I did for ten years.

I survived personality disorders, dysfunctional behaviors, threats, bullying, defamation, discrimination, suppression, and oppression. The Negative Nancys and Debbie Downers of the 20th century were no match for the Creepers, Squatters, Ice Queens, Florals, Blockheads, Medusas, Jekylls and Hydes, and Locusts in addition to the many con artists and liars embedded in toxic cultures in the workplaces I experienced.

The Circus had many other acts and performances I did not mention in the previous chapters that further contributed to the toxic environment. There were various sex scandals involving directors, facilitators, staff, visitors, alumni, community partners, program participants, and interns, in which some led to pregnancies while others led to promotions or volatile relationships. The affairs had by married individuals resulted in lawsuits and physical altercations while inappropriate private parties and quid pro quo led to increased salaries and permanent/untouchable job positions. Sexual harassment claims were overlooked and were in the hands of the victim if they wanted some relief. I remember specifically being harassed by a photographer as an intern and being told "oh he says that to every woman, just ignore him" and as it progressed, I had to make threats to him in order to end the disgusting remarks and inappropriate touches. Plans of conspiring to get executives fired and to seek power became unfortunate common news, while firings due to embezzlement plagued the organization, including the HR representative who was supposed to assist me from the hostile environment of Jekyll's regime. The sad part is the toxicity still continues in this environment to this day...same play different actors.

I'm a Survivor

In reflection, I can conclude life has a funny way of preparing us for our future. In Chapter One, the assessment of my environment, as a child, in my consideration of attainable career aspirations was a natural process. I ruled out careers placed upon me, questioned intangible suggestions and pondered dreams for suitable pursuits. Gottredson's theory of circumscription, compromise, and self-creation insinuates as a person matures through the stages of life from childhood through early adulthood, they begin to compromise their career aspirations due to social inequalities they perceive for themselves based on how they view their parents and elements of their upbringing. Through this time period, we are soaking in patterns, imitating gestures and emotions, adopting values and mindsets, developing habits and personalities, negotiating character traits, and trying on experiences all while discovering ourselves as we process who we are to become.

I firmly believe nothing is wasted and everything we experience has its place in our life's journey. The good and bad, the positive and negative, the beautiful and ugly, all matter in shaping our identity. An identity we are constantly seeking to feed through associations and affiliations within our familial circles and beyond. We search for jobs and careers to reflect who we are or who we desire to become. This exploration is all rooted in the familial relationships, environments, socioeconomic statuses, and educational experiences we encounter growing up, which ultimately affect how we approach our career choices and academic pursuits as adults.

The familial influence is one of the strongest psychological constructs in our matriculation from childhood to adulthood. Therefore, the given environments comprising the people, places, and experiences in our childhood are not happenstance but Greecian columns and fractal mazes chosen for the fabric of our essence. How we learn from our history and navigate through our trials is the freedom we have in the construction of self.

My understanding of who I was to become required the familial influences, childhood experiences, and tough work situations I had to endure on my path to early adulthood. The joys and the pains were necessary to reach the shores of opportunities and walk through doors of success destined for me. These years built my muscle and trained my mind for endurance through all tests, trials, and victories that would come in the interlocking cycles to accomplish my professional goals and live out my dreams.

The workplace is a uniquely rich, dynamic environment in its ability to develop, provide, produce, unite, destroy, invoke, hurt, and guide people, dreams, and livelihoods. The majority of our days as adults are spent at work and a significant part of our lives are tied to our jobs. Our very identities are linked in the work we do and the careers we pursue. Our dreams of every age are enacted in the workplace. The place where we work is not limited to office walls, it's courtrooms, athletic courts, parks, malls, stadiums, camps, streets, restaurants, community centers, schools, stations, hotels, boats/ships, stages, planes, yards, churches, homes, and in hearts and minds. No matter what we call the workplace, it is our environment and plays a significant role in our evolution.

In Chapter Two, I was fortunate to experience a positive work environment which was pivotal in my learning what work could be like, so that I would not accept the future negative environments as the norm. It taught me that workplaces should prioritize the safety of their employees and be genuinely concerned about their growth and overall well being. Since writing this book, I have not only been in continuous positive work environments but also served on committees to promote employee relations. This has helped tremendously in processing the hurt from the toxicity and diverting its remnants into positivity.

I had to learn in my new environment, though everything may not be positive, does not make it a toxic atmosphere. In any workplace, there are going to be disagreements, disappointments, and dissatisfactions. The negative effects toxic environments have on you can be everlasting but you cannot let your old wounds ignite the automatic defense mechanisms in your new situations.

Everyone cannot be pleased all the time, but employers can create an environment that is fair and accommodating. Communication, just like in any relationship, is king. An organization that practices transparency, fosters employee growth, cognizant of work-life situations, assumes social responsibility, and practices consistency in their messaging will be a well sought after employer. Understanding the correlation of productivity and satisfaction to generate mutually beneficial relationships with employees, will be the driving force to creating and maintaining a pleasant workplace.

My experiences with toxicity helped me to appreciate the simple things and matured me. Being the butt of jokes, discriminated against, and mistreated helped me to be more empathetic. As a child I was mature for my age because I had the pleasure of keeping company with older adults. However, somehow as a young adult, at times I found myself easily persuaded to join in on meaningless gossip and the talking bad about an individual as a pastime. When you are in those shoes, you realize this behavior is harmful and insensitive. Contributing to forms of relational aggression is a toxic behavior and knowing you are better than those you have survived, becomes a quick wake up call.

Having gone through toxic situations should be a badge of honor. The lessons it has taught you are needed no matter where your feet land. You should never lose your voice and always be ready to stand your ground. Never get comfortable with the status quo just because things are "good" but strive for greatness. Be a change agent and do not lose the edge the toxicity gave you; however, exercise patience and seek understanding before reacting.

One of the biggest lessons I learned in working in toxic environments was separating the dysfunctional behavior from the person displaying the behavior. It becomes so easy to label a person based on their personality and how they act. I know, I gave them nicknames in this book. However, I had to put myself in their shoes and think about how I would hate to be labeled with a negative connotation because that means I would be bound to that characteristic no matter what my evolution brought. Recognizing this separation also helped me to not hold grudges, which is beneficial to my health and well-being. I've heard it several times before and you probably have also, "unforgiveness is like drinking poison and expecting the other person to die". The emotions we experience in toxic environments cause us to formulate opinions and dislikes of people and that is perfectly healthy. However, it's the grudges and the animosity we choose to hold that cause a dis-ease in our body. So take deep breaths thinking of all the hurt, pain, embarrassment, behaviors, and anger of the toxicity and exhale to release these toxins from your mind, body, and spirit.

Another way to purge the toxicity is to talk about it while you're going through it and afterwards. The significance of having workplace friendships is just not for the benefit of organizational performance but the sanity of mankind. Being able to emote to a trustworthy person is healthy in pushing the toxins out as it lends to alliances needed to battle the toxicity and garner support, advice, and solutions. You have to release the poison and having someone to listen as you talk the situation out can be pivotal in discovering how to better handle future challenges and draw attention to needed assistance.

Remember in my Watchmens story, I released that toxicity into a letter to the regional manager and as a result, the harassment stopped. Had I not, then the feeling of oppression would have continued to manifest itself in my and the other affected folks in my department. At some point, you have to escalate the venting sessions if you truly want peace. Much change can happen when a group centered on a cause addresses the concerns, there is definitely power in numbers, but it starts with building healthy relationships with individuals.

This constant sounding board will help in the day-to-day operations. Other ways are to take breaks, get some fresh air, or sometimes just relax to some uplifting music that allows you to mentally escape for a few minutes. However you choose to positively release is great as long as you are releasing. When you get to the point you can talk about a situation without dredging up the emotions tied to it, then you know you have overcome. Remember, it is your sanity that is at stake here and you cannot let toxic managers, co-workers, and associates drain your energy nor compromise your sanity.

There are times you will need to speak to the toxic person and having that workplace friend will help you to practice before your conversation. You will want to make sure you are following the guidelines as related to dealing with their specific disorder and check your emotions at the door. Additionally, documentation is another two-fold way to vent. Immediately recording the situations helps in the purging process and helps to record the specifics of the interactions, which you may need later. If you journal, maybe consider having a PG version for your documentation so as not to mix your true feelings in the workplace documentation that may need to be submitted to HR, should there be a case. Remember communication is key, talk it out, whether it be to a friend or ally and write it out, because if you need it later, it never existed unless it was documented.

In Chapter Four, we learned about the rise and fall of workplace relationships and how the mere existence of workplace cliques can cause isolation and ostracism. Establishing workplace friendships are a must and everyone needs them for sanity, even if you are insane. From these relationships, I believe you will learn a lot about yourself and others by who you or they decide to associate with and for what reason. I encourage you to not only seek positive relationships but determine how the relationship can invoke change to improve your current environment. Afterall, love is the antidote to hate. Having a positive work friendship does not keep you in the loop of what is going on, but when you are able to share information and express your frustrations, it is a way to detox.

The workplace relationships I acquired helped me in my personal life as well. Danille and I are still friends to this day and we keep tabs on what is happening in our old workplace, though both of us are far removed. There are seasons when our time may end at a work environment but life may bring us back and that is where our friendships can be beneficial.

The song says "life is but a dream" and in toxic environments it is your dreams that should be the boat rowing you right on out. Our imaginations or even our subconscious is filled with things we can't explain and pathways to obtainable visions. The Bible says 'God will always provide a way of escape in compromising situations' and sometimes that could be in the form of our minds. Our dreams can be the driving force to lead us out of situations, to make us want for more, it's our dangling carrot.

I believe that if the dream is there, it is worth pursuing. Though it may get deferred, like the many times I shared how mine were, I never gave up believing in them. As life went on, my path may have changed a bit but I did not lose the dream, I just reshaped it. After several real life situations, I realized I no longer sought refuge in a rich athlete husband but I would be fine with handling the household and running businesses with partners and my husband, no matter his athleticism. The fact was I saw the professional athlete as the quickest boat out of the situation but as I matured and grew into other environments, I learned about other types of boats.

There were also other types of barriers that came with each triumph and new opportunity. Sometimes these barriers were in the form of battles divinely designed to develop the skills I needed to survive the next obstacle on my road to victory. The shams and scams were just warm ups. What I learned is we have larger battles than what we physically see.

In the workplace, there are policies that reflect institutional discrimination, further demonstrating that it is not the people we need to be mad at but the created systems. We need to align and bring attention to the discriminatory processes. Yes the system is made to keep certain people down, but it is not always purposefully. You can only expect people to develop rules and regulations based on their perspective, so naturally, policies will reflect the biases of its author. What we have to understand is our duty to ensure that the governing bodies understand the discriminatory principles in order to revise the process to be inclusive of all. This will be a revolving cycle as time goes on. We will each learn and discover the various nuances of the human race as humanity evolves. If in the event there is no longer a fit and the toxicity is unbearable, remember you have a boat, so get on it and let it take you to another world.

Chapters Six through Nine chronicled my personal encounters with bearers of personality disorders and difficult behaviors that led to my survival mantra, "It's me, not you". Being able to rise above the toxicity involved me learning more about myself to recognize what I truly wanted in life. It was pivotal to my sanity to understand that my desire for peace and freedom were intangibles that surpassed the walls of the workplace.

Toxicity comes in many forms and patterns that perpetuate the environment. It is not just the personality disorders and difficult behaviors that lead to the overall dysfunction but the systematic and cultural biases from the outside that influence the individuals who make up the toxic work environment. The majority of my instances came from those who were in executive positions who were fine examples of the top down management approach. What I had to realize was the discrimination, bullying, and acts of relational aggression were not just reflections of the culture but were also remnants of their negative past experiences, many stemming from their childhood.

When I mentioned in previous chapters how you have to separate the behavior from the person, it is a level of maturity of understanding that the healing of a hurt person can ultimately change the quality of their human interaction. Also be cognizant that certain behaviors trigger negative reactions and cause relapses in individuals, so acknowledging "It's me, not you" helps you to exercise grace towards someone who is suffering. It also assists you in avoiding being a hostage of the venomous atmosphere.

What I hope you are able to walk away knowing is that just because it may be a war at your workplace, you do not have to fight nor engage in every battle. You'll get tired and ultimately lose because they will get the best of you. You have to set your mind on higher things, such as your vision and purpose. Don't come out of character to prove anything to anyone, be secure in knowing you are great and have great things ahead of you that you cannot jeopardize over pettiness. The more you stand firm in who you are, the more you will realize the battle is not yours but the one they struggle with within themselves.

Yes, it's hard, especially when you feel you are often being tested but when you hold yourself responsible for your actions then you can say "It's me, not you" and walk away. I know it's their fault, yes they are dead wrong, but you have the power to dictate your reaction and if you choose not to participate in negativity, then you won't. Taking ownership gives YOU the power, not them. As soon as you give them power to control the situation by saying 'you started it, it is your fault', you have just given them permission to torment you. Choose to stick to the facts and filter your emotions from the interaction; your sanity depends on it.

I have never proclaimed myself to be totally innocent in my experience. I recognize my mistakes, shortcomings, and vengeance. I have given pieces of my mind away just for it not to change anything or anyone. Naturally I could have prevented a lot of things had I been properly trained to be a manager but life is about learning and my trial and error work experience has been a good teacher. The people I worked with had some toxic personalities, but there were things I could have done differently to not have been toxified, that is why I take the blame for my behavior for dealing with them generally and not specifically for their personality disorder.

That is the key to survival in toxic environments. You may not necessarily be able to change the entire environment because environments are deeply rooted in an established culture well before you and your colleagues came along. The purpose of this book and the stories was to recognize the toxicity and not to accept it as the way things have always been nor for you to put on your cape to take on Gotham City. This collection of stories was to help you identify the disorders and discover ways you can handle the toxicity to avoid being a casualty or perpetuator of the environment. My hope is this book helps you to learn from my mistakes and reflect on your similar experiences in order to deal with toxicity, while keeping your sanity until you can leave.

Survivor Guilt

Survivor guilt is a condition usually associated with those who have lost a loved one, especially in a traumatic situation where they survived and another person(s) did not. It is a sense of feeling guilty that another person lost their life while yours was spared. It can often lead to depression, nightmares, fear, helplessness, or disconnection. Survivor guilt also translates to other situations beyond death, such as the workplace. When leaving a toxic work environment, you may feel bad in leaving your allies and/or friends behind to fend for themselves as you move onto greater things. You definitely do not want to abandon them but the probability of everyone getting a new job and leaving at the same time is low. It is at this point, though you are not physically there, you can be their motivation and outlet until their time to leave comes.

Another way survivor guilt can be experienced in the workplace is in the mistreatment of certain individuals. For example, Danille had survivor guilt when Jekyll's wrath shifted to me instead of her, once Jekyll realized firing the budget administrator could be detrimental. Danille had expressed her guilt to me, stating she knew the animosity was meant for her and she would at times apologize to me for what I experienced at the hands of Jekyll. I assured her it was not her fault, she was not treating me badly nor did she play any part. It was an unfortunate situation but it further proves the magnitude of a toxic environment. It not only affects people directly but others who witness these acts and often fear they could be the next target.

There is no solace in toxic work environments and no one comes out unscathed. If you choose to stay then make the best of your situation and gain allies and emote to a trusted source(s) to release the toxins you inhale from just being present in the atmosphere. If you want out, then make every effort to exit and be the inspiration for those who are awaiting their departure. Until you are able to make your move, know that you are not alone in what you experience and light is at the end of the tunnel. Nothing lasts forever...your journey starts and ends with you, so always choose you.

AFTERWORD

The incomparable Whitney Houston once sang the infamous words, "For every win someone must fail, but there comes a point when, when we exhale". I write to you now exhaling from the experiences in this book and from its completion. To think this project has been in the making since I first had my toxic encounter and the fact I kept my emails and notes from years prior, knowing they would serve a purpose someday, is the mystic of life. I count it all joy knowing through my failures there were victories for me and for others. Nothing in life is wasted, not even old emails; everything has a purpose in its time.

After my season ended at The Circus, I went back to school and earned a doctorate where my research interest evolved into career development, with a concentration on family career legacies. Since graduating, I have spoken at various national and international conferences on my research and enjoyed every moment. I have written chapters for a couple academic book series and have even dabbled in fiction. Being able to combine my scholastic knowledge with my practical work experience through my writing and consulting has come full circle. It has allowed me to provide support and guidance to help people be better in their professional and personal lives.

All that I have gone through has not been in vain. It did take me a while to process the hurt I felt from all of the environments, but though I have my scars, I am no longer wounded. Furthering my education was enlightening because it led me to freedom and from the freedom I found peace. My emotional scars from toxicity are only reminders of my growing pains which were necessary to move me into my purpose.

Writing this book was not easy because it required me to dredge up some suppressed memories, revisit some ugly situations, and reveal a few secrets. However, I found it to be an incredible release because this book had literally taken residence in my mind for many years, so to evict it was a commencement. I now have the capacity to proceed with other writing projects that will add to my body of work.

It's Me, Not You challenged me so that it could help you, the reader. I am truly excited about being able to share the stories from this career autobiography through various platforms. I also look forward to hearing the multitude of stories from people who this book was ordained to reach. I am and will remain an ally to those who are in the struggle of the toxic work environment. The mere thought of knowing this book was by divine design makes me feel honored to have been chosen to deliver a message of encouragement and self-reflection. I hope *It's Me, Not You* has been resourceful, ignited self-reflection, and made you giggle a little. It has been an absolute joy to document these experiences over the past couple of years. I am excited to be on this legacy journey as I move on to my next chapter in life and am grateful to you for being a part of it. Be blessed!

Sincerely,

Dr. PJ
Porscha Jackson, PhD
info@drpj.online
www.drpj.online

REFERENCES

Chope, R. (2006). Family Matters: The influence of the family in career decision making. Austin, TX: Pro Ed.

Crothers, L. M., Lipinski, J., & Minutolo, M. C. (2009). Cliques, rumors, and gossip by the water cooler: Female bullying in the workplace. The Psychologist-Manager Journal, 12(2), 97–110. https://doi.org/10.1080/10887150902886423

Degges-White, S. (2017, December 15). The top 10 personality disorders: Symptoms & signs. Psychology Today. Retrieved from www.psychologytoday.com

Dickie, C. (2009). Exploring Workplace Friendships in Business: Cultural Variations of Employee Behaviour. Research and Practice in Human Resource Management, 17(1), 128-137.

Fine, G. A. (1986). Friendships in the workplace. In V. Derlaga, & B. Winstead (Eds.), Friendship and Social Interaction (pp. 185-206). Springer-Verlag.

Gottfredson, L.S. (2002). Gottfredson's theory of circumscription, compromise, and self
creation. In D. Brown & Associates (Eds.), Career choice and development (4th
ed., p. 85-148). San Francisco: Jossey-Bass.

Hall, D. (2002). Careers in and out of organizations. Thousand Oaks, CA: Sage
Publications. Inc.

Harris, J. I., Winskowski, A. M., & Engdahl, B. E. (2007). Types of workplace social support in the prediction of job satisfaction. The Career Development Quarterly, 56(2), 150–156. https://doi.org/10.1002/j.2161-0045.2007.tb00027.x

Jackson, P. (2020). Under the influence: The familial construction of career identity. In S. Motulsky, J. Gammel, & A. Rutstein-Riley (Eds.), Identity & lifelong learning: Becoming through lived experience, (pp.221-242). Charlotte, NC: Information Age Publishing, Inc.

Jackson, P.R. (2016). A tale of two legacies: Career narratives of the black family business. Journal Black Studies, 47(1), 53-72.

Jackson, P.R. (2014). Family careers reloaded: Lessons for the 21st century workforce (Doctoral dissertation, Texas A&M University). Retrieved: http://oaktrust.library.tamu.edu/handle/1969.1/153953

Kusy, M., & Holloway, E. (2009). Toxic workplace!: managing toxic personalities and their systems of power. San Francisco, Jossey-Bass.

Leavitt, K., & Sluss, D. M. (2015). Lying for who we are: An identity-based model of workplace dishonesty. The Academy of Management Review, 40(4), 587–610. https://doi.org/10.5465/amr.2013.0167

Lubit, R. (2004). The tyranny of toxic managers: Applying emotional intelligence to deal with difficult personalities. Ivey Business Journal, 1-7 March-April.

Lutgen-Sandvik, P. (2006). Take this job and ...: Quitting and other forms of resistance to workplace bullying. Communication Monographs, 73(4), 406–433. https://doi.org/10.1080/03637750601024156

Mao, H., Hsieh, A., & Chen, C. (2012). The relationship between workplace friendship and perceived job significance. Journal of Management & Organization, 18, 247-262.

Marson, S. & Hessmiller, J. (2016). The dark side of being pretty. Journal of Sociology and Social Work, 4(1), 58-67.

McAndrew, F. T. (2014). The "sword of a woman": Gossip and female aggression. Aggression and Violent Behavior, 19(3), 196–199. https://doi.org/10.1016/j.avb.2014.04.006

Miller-Ott, A. E., & Kelly, L. (2013). Mean Girls in College: An Analysis of How College Women Communicatively Construct and Account for Relational Aggression. Women's Studies in Communication, 36(3), 330–347. https://doi.org/10.1080/07491409.2013.829792

Mitchell, T. R., Holtom, B. C., Lee, T. W., Sablynski, C. J., & Erez, M. (2001). Why people stay: Using job embeddedness to predict voluntary turnover. Academy of Management Journal, 44(6), 1102–1121. https://doi.org/10.2307/3069391

Morrison, R. L. (2009). Are women tending and befriending in the workplace?

Gender differences in the relationship between workplace friendships and organizational outcomes. Sex Roles: A Journal of Research, 60(1-2), 1–13. https://doi.org/10.1007/s11199-008-9513-4

Palting, H.C. (2016). Adult relational aggression. Hubpages.com/relationships/adult-relational-aggression. HubPages, May 25, 2018 retrieved.

Sachs, L. (2013, August 28). How to deal with paranoia in the workplace. CM Crossroads. Retrieved from cmcrossroads.com/article/how-deal-paranoia-workplace

Schneider, B. (1987). The people make the place. Personnel Psychology, 40(3), 437–453. https://doi.org/10.1111/j.1744-6570.1987.tb00609.x

Schneider, B. (1983). Interactional psychology and organizational behavior. Research in Organizational Behavior, 5, 1–31.

Schwartz, Stanley J. (1993). Insubordination: A cardinal sin in the workplace. Labor Law Journal; Chicago Vol. 44, Iss. 12, (Dec 1, 1993): 765.

Sias, P.M. (2009). Social Ostracism, Cliques, and Outcasts. Destructive organizational communication: Processes, consequences, & constructive ways of organizing, 145-163.

Sias, P. M., Heath, R. G., Perry, T., Silva, D., & Fix, B. (2004). Narratives of workplace friendship deterioration. Journal of Social and Personal Relationships, 21(3), 321–340. https://doi.org/10.1177/0265407504042835

Sluss, D. M., van Dick, R., & Thompson, B. S. (2011). Role theory in organizations: A relational perspective. In S. Zedeck (Ed.), APA handbook of industrial and organizational psychology, Vol. 1. Building and developing the organization (pp. 505–534). American Psychological Association. https://doi.org/10.1037/12169-016

Song, S.-H., & Olshfski, D. (2008). Friends at work: A comparative study of work attitudes in Seoul city government and New Jersey state government. Administration & Society, 40(2), 147–169. https://doi.org/10.1177/0095399707312827

Stamarski, C. S., & Son Hing, L. S. (2015). Gender inequalities in the workplace: The effects of organizational structures, processes, practices, and decision makers' sexism. Frontiers in Psychology, 6, Article 1400. https://doi.org/10.3389/fpsyg.2015.01400

Tews, M. J., Michel, J. W., & Allen, D. G. (2014). Fun and friends: The impact of workplace fun and constituent attachment on turnover in a hospitality context. Human Relations, 67(8), 923–946. https://doi.org/10.1177/0018726713508143

WebMD, (2020, May 31) Paranoid personality disorder. Retrieved from webmd.com/mental-health/paranoid-personality-disorder#1

Whiston, S. C., & Keller, B. K. (2004). The Influences of the Family of Origin on Career Development: A Review and Analysis. The Counseling Psychologist, 32(4), 493–568. https://doi.org/10.1177/0011000004265660

ABOUT THE AUTHOR

Porscha "Dr. PJ" Jackson, PhD is a career consultant, small business advocate and author of Pursuing Legacy: Principles for an Influential Life & Impactful Career, an informative and encouraging guide on building career legacies and It's Me, Not You: How I Survived Toxic Work Environments. She has also contributed chapters to: Sisterhood Story (a fictional anthology produced by Delta Sigma Theta Sorority, Inc.); Global Perspectives on Issues and Solutions in Urban Education (an academic text on scholarly and practical solutions for urban environments); and I am What I Become (a volume series on identity and lifelong learning).

During her doctoral candidacy in human resource development, she developed an interest in the familial influence on careers and has since become a field expert in the research of career legacies and its parallelism to workforce development. Grounded in her mission of "helping people become better versions of themselves", Dr. PJ is an advocate for historically disenfranchised firms and the career development of marginalized individuals. Throughout her career, she has received awards for her work in the community and is highly recognized and respected for her professionalism, project management accomplishments, and national conference presentations and keynotes on career-related issues and personnel and business development.

Dr. PJ enjoys bringing to light untold stories in her writings and YouTube show, Dr. PJ's StoryLine. Outside of her profession, she is an avid traveler and dessert aficionado, who seeks adventure and cultural exploration in her leisure.

Additionally, she is actively involved in various community and professional organizations centered on human resource development, adult learning, and urban education. She also enjoys advocating for Successful Shoes, a 501 (c) 3 nonprofit organization she founded to provide encouragement and support through shoe donations and career development services to women in transitional programs and facilities.